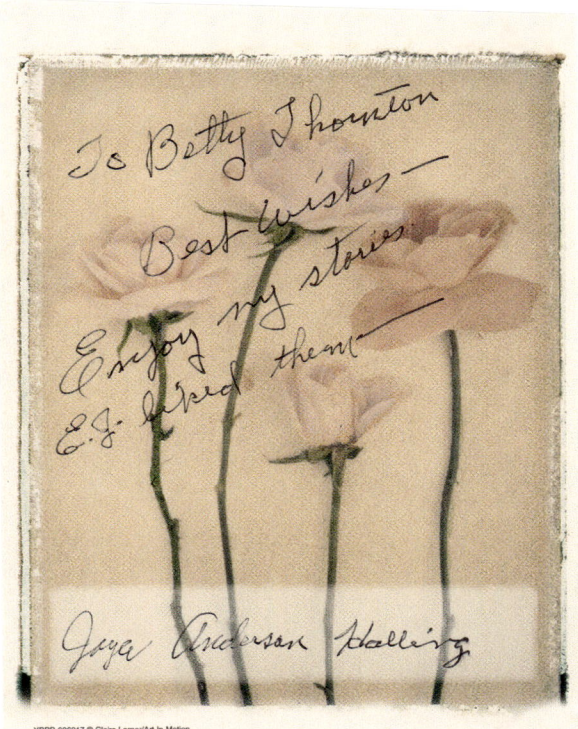

To Betty Thornton

Best wishes—

Enjoy my stories.

E.J. liked them—

Joya Anderson Halling

YBPP-606017 © Claire Lerner/Art In Motion

Growing Up in the 1930s

A Memoir of Childhood in Perry, Iowa

Joyce Anderson Halling

All places, people, and events mentioned in this book are accurate as to Perry, Iowa, in the 1930s. The reader will forgive any discrepancies with the regrets of the author.

Published by:
Amy J. Beveridge
435 Main St.
Bellville, OH 44813

Printed in the United States of America.

ISBN 0-9786751-0-X

12 11 10 09 08 07 06   9 8 7 6 5 4 3 2 1

Library of Congress Control Number: 2006927856

Contents

Acknowledgements

Special thanks to the citizens of Perry, and the surrounding communities, for making central Iowa such a delightful place to live.

Thanks to my teacher, Mary Theresa Fallon, for her wisdom, gentle correction, guidance, and encouragement to continue writing.

Thanks to my friends who made childhood such a special time.

Thanks to my family for their love and support.

Thanks to my parents, Ruby McArthur and Marion Anderson, for doing their best to provide for five children during the Great Depression.

Finally, thanks to my brothers, George, John, and Dennis, for the memories.

Summer

Summer Fun at Pattee Park

During the summer, I think every child in town spent time in Pattee Park, either by playing on the playground equipment, climbing on the old World War I cannon with its large wheels, or looking for crawdads in Frog Creek. But by far the most popular place to be was at the swimming pool.

At that time, this concrete pool was the only one in Perry. It had a large bathhouse, with separate changing rooms for boys and girls. These changing rooms had hooks mounted on the walls where swimmers could hang their clothes, with space on the floor for shoes. (A few years later, after a new bathhouse was constructed, swimmers were given numbered pins and baskets in which to place their clothes and shoes.) Although there were enough changing stalls to accommodate everyone, most children came to the pool wearing their suits, and carried their dry clothing rolled in their towels.

After changing or depositing one's clothes, each swimmer was required to pass through the "shower" before entering the swimming area. This "shower" sprayed cold water from all sides of an open stall. Swimmers had to get their suits wet or absolutely freeze when entering the water.

3

There also was a large pan on the floor containing disinfectant. One also had to step into this before leaving the dressing room. It was not unusual to see children scrubbing their feet in an adjacent bucket of water because they got them so dirty walking barefoot to the pool on the gravel road. Outside around the pool was a concrete walkway with several benches.

A rope separated the two-foot area from the three- to four-foot area. Beyond this, another rope separated this area from the five-foot area, and yet another rope beyond this designated the deepest water, which was ten feet. There were diving boards at the south end. In the two-foot area, there was a step down into the water that ran across the north end of the pool from east to west. I often entered the pool using this step, as it was smooth to walk on. There was quite a bit of tar patching in this area, unlike the rough concrete surface covering the rest of the pool's bottom.

The first week or so that the pool was open, the water would be halfway clear and as cold as ice. Then the water turned a murky-green and you could not see your hands or feet in it. Several times during the summer, the water had to be drained so the pool could be cleaned. One time I remember seeing Barton Fitzgerald, a lifeguard, repeatedly diving into the four-foot area. After several attempts, he came up with a large turtle someone had probably thrown over the fence the night before! The poor turtle never had a chance in the chlorinated water.

Each year on opening day, Daddy would drive my brothers and me in his 1929 Model A Ford pickup down to the pool to purchase our season passes, which were fifty cents apiece. We all knew how to swim because our dad had insisted we participate in Red Cross swim lessons. Over the course of several weeks, we learned how to swim and how to dive into the water from the side of the pool. (Any antics performed on the diving board or towers, however, were always self-taught!)

We loved going to the pool. It was fourteen blocks from our house on Seventh and North to the entrance of the park on Willis and West Third. We always cut through Pattee Park diagonally, crossing Frog Creek on the little footbridge. The closer we came to the pool, the stronger the smell of chlorine became. How exciting to experience that smell again! But, after playing most of the afternoon in the pool, the walk home was torture. On the way home, we would stop at Mrs. Council's popcorn stand to beg for "old maids." She loved children and always gave us a little extra popped corn on top. I suspect she knew most of the children in Perry. The Milwaukee Depot was located on Second between Bateman and Rawson Streets. Often Denny and I would stop at the depot, take off our shoes, and walk barefoot on the rails to Sixth Street. Sometimes the rails were so hot they burned my feet! I quickly learned how to walk the rails wearing my leather-soled shoes.

Arriving home, there were wet suits and towels that needed attention. We were each responsible for our own. When this chore was completed, we collapsed in complete exhaustion on the living room floor to wait for supper to revive us. I don't ever remember being as tired as I was after an afternoon at the pool.

An Adventure
at Black Bridge

In June of 1932, Dennis was six, I was eight, John was ten, and George was twelve. Our mother was in the hospital with a newborn and she was very ill. Our father had dismissed the hired girl so he was "batching" it with four children. While Daddy was at work, Denny and I were being "bossed" by our older brothers. They took their duties seriously and never left us alone.

Early one morning Daddy decided to clean the house. After breakfast he gave each of us a paperhanging brush and on our hands and knees, we brushed all the downstairs window sills, woodwork, and floors. Daddy followed us closely, sweeping up the accumulation of dust and dirt. If we missed something we received a gentle reminder on our bottoms from Daddy's broom! When we were finished downstairs, he gave the dust mop and dust cloths to George and John and sent them upstairs to clean and to make the beds. Daddy had cleaned most of the bathroom before we got up, but had left the sink for me to clean while he scrubbed the kitchen floor.

After Daddy left for work, George and John made cold meat sandwiches with pickle and pimento, my favorite! They also made some iced tea. Carefully they put all the sandwiches in a paper sack, poured the tea into a large pitcher, and put everything in the icebox. They hung a sign on the door that said, "Keep Out or Else!" Daddy came home at noon to eat and to check on us. Assured that John and George had everything under control, he returned to work.

That afternoon the boys decided to go to Black Bridge, which was (and still is) an old iron bridge that spans Beaver Creek north of Perry. It was a long, hot walk for short legs, but I'd heard so much about playing in the creek that I was anxious to trudge along behind the boys. Along the way, we checked for gopher and snake holes, and we picked a few violets growing along the roadside. We watched a chicken hawk slowly circle overhead and heard the rumpus and squawking of some nearby chickens running in a farmer's yard.

The bridge was at the bottom of a long, curving hill, and I noticed the water was very low in the creek bed. In fact, there was hardly any water at all. This was unusual for June. Both John and George climbed onto the bridge, stood up, and then walked across to the top. I thought that looked like a lot of fun, so I too crawled up, but, not being as brave as my older brothers, I straddled the bridge and scooted to the top. I stopped to look around and was quite impressed with all I could see from the top of the bridge. Then I looked down.

I think it was probably twenty-five feet to the creek bed. Suddenly, all the awe and wonderment I'd just experienced was pushed aside as fear took control of me. My breath caught in my throat, something squeezed my stomach, and my legs started shaking. I leaned down on my stomach, wrapped my legs and arms around the girder, and held on as tightly as I could. My heart was pounding so hard, I could not only hear it but also I could feel the blood coursing through my arms and legs. Because I froze, Denny also became frightened and hung on for dear life!

George and John were able to talk Denny down first, but talking didn't do much for me. I cried as George pushed on my shoulders and John pulled on my hips. The more they pushed and pulled, the tighter I held on, and the louder I wailed! After awhile I opened my eyes and just stared at the black paint on the bridge under my face. It had a queer smell, sort of a dirty metal odor. I could see the feet and legs of one of my brothers.

George knelt down, placed his face very close to mine and whispered, "If you just let go a little bit Joyce, we will slide you down the girder to where your feet can touch the crossbars."

I closed my eyes, loosened my grip, and felt myself sliding along the top of the bridge. After a gradual slope down, my right foot felt the crossbars, and I stepped off the bridge. Even though both George and John said they would never, ever take me with them again, it wasn't long before I found myself again in their company at Black Bridge.

Flies on the Screen Door

One day I ran across the front porch and out the front door. *Whap!* went the screen door behind me.

"Joyce," my father called, "come back here and go out that door like you're supposed to."

"Yes, Daddy." I slowly came back indoors, carefully opening and closing the screen door. I turned around and went back out the door, silently closing the screen door behind me.

"That's better. Try to remember how to open and close a screen door, especially when there are flies on it!"

"Yes, Daddy. I'll remember."

About then George, John, and Denny, spaced several feet apart, came running out the front door. The three resulting *whaps* were preceded by three cracking sounds of the screen door hitting the side of the house. Our dad jumped to his feet, stepped outdoors, and called the three of them back to run them through the "proper" routine of opening and closing a screen door.

We all honestly tried to open and close the door as Daddy wanted us to do, but sometimes when we were in a hurry it was easy to forget and be halfway down the front steps before the *whap* noise reminded us we forgot it, again.

That night I overheard Daddy tell Momma about an attachment that could be put on the screen door to keep the noise down. It was a rubber ball extended on a heavy wire-like piece that could be screwed into the edge of the doorframe.

"It's supposed to make the door closing less noisy," said my dad.

"I'm willing to try anything," said Momma. "I'll also repair the hole that someone poked into the new screen!"

The next morning Momma called me to go with her out to the garage. "You are going to help me repair that hole in the screen door. Did you ever notice how a fly will land on the screen and keep walking around until he finds an opening to get into the house?"

"Yes, I've seen a fly come through the hole," I answered.

"Well, we're going to close off his entryway!"

She cut a piece from a roll of screen larger than the hole, and then pulled loose a long wire from a raw cut edge of the roll. With wire in hand, we headed for the front door.

Momma put me inside the door and laid the patch over the hole. She poked the wire through both the patch and the screen, then told me I was to pull it through. I did as she said and then poked the wire back through the screen to her side. We kept "sewing" with the wire until we were around the outside edge and the patch was firmly held by our stitches.

"I don't think Mr. Fly will get through that hole again," said Momma.

I giggled at the thought of a fly trying to get into the house!

12

Daddy came home from work about five o'clock and handed Momma a little sack. In it was the rubber ball attached to a short wire. After supper Daddy took his screwdriver and affixed the little contraption to the inside of the screen door, very close to the edge, about eighteen inches from the top of the door.

"John," Daddy called, "come here and go out the front door fast!"

"But you'll get after me," he said.

"No, John, not this time. I want to see if this thing works."

John obliged, but didn't push the door so hard it would touch the house before it closed. He let go of it and the door swung back into place. It bounced open about twelve inches, closed again, bounced about four inches, and then settled in.

The *whap* of the screen door was no longer heard at our house. Momma and Daddy were greatly pleased with the sudden reduction of noise. But a fly problem remained! Every time Momma started cooking, the flies would swarm around the screen door. No matter how careful we children were, each time we opened the screen door, a few would fly in.

One afternoon Momma said, "I can't put supper on the table. There are so many flies in this house it makes me sick!"

My dad had the solution to this problem. He cut each of us children and himself a tree branch with quite a few leaves on it. He sent us upstairs to "herd" the flies out. We started in my room, the east bedroom. My how we swung those branches around! In every nook and corner of the room, we vigorously shook them.

George and John waited in the hall and when Denny and I reached the door they went into action swinging their branches and shooing the flies down the hall. I closed my bedroom door. We repeated this in the other two bedrooms and chased the flies downstairs. Denny and I stood at the bottom of the stairs swishing our branches back and forth so they could not come back up the stairway, while George, John, and Daddy ran them out the front door. When we were finished there wasn't a single fly in the house!

At this point we children were given a choice: either to go outdoors or to play in the house, but no more running back and forth. We chose to stay in and listen to the radio until supper was on the table.

Momma said, "That was a fast way of clearing out the flies. But it would be so much simpler if we would just chase them away at the door as we come in or out."

Dutifully we tried to remember, but to us children, the excitement of going outdoors was a greater pull on our attention.

The screen door didn't *whap* anymore, but its *bounce-bounce* did let in a few flies at a time. Take however many times a child goes in and out a door, and multiply that by four, and you can easily see that the call for the "Branch Brigade" was soon upon us again!

Summer Rainstorm

Sometimes in the summer, a rainstorm would move in. Often it was preceded by very strong winds. When a storm was approaching, we children would scurry around gathering the yard chairs to bring into the house. Denny, John, and George would help me carry my playhouse furniture into the garage to keep it from blowing away. If Momma had anything on the wash line, she hurriedly removed it, and my dad would drive his pickup into the garage.

One evening such a storm blew in. Momma sat in the bay window with Denny on one knee and me on the other so we could watch the storm. There was an exceedingly tall oak tree between our house and Goodwins' to the east. I was afraid of this tree because the branches and leaves would whip menacingly back and forth whenever a storm was coming. They seemed to shake at me, jump at me, and even reach down towards me. I knew someday they would get me for sure! But this time the tree couldn't get me because Momma's lap was a safe place to be whenever I felt threatened.

Each time the lightning flashed, it illuminated the entire neighborhood. The lightning scared Denny and me, so Momma said,

"Did you see that squirrel by the tree?"

Denny and I both said, "No!"

Momma said, "The next time the lightning flashes, look at the foot of the tree."

As the lightning continued, she would call various things to our attention. We were so engrossed in looking for these things, we eventually slipped off her lap and stood closer to the window to see. Suddenly an enormous clap of thunder shook the house and Denny and I jumped back onto Momma's lap.

"It's coming, it's coming!" I shouted.

"What's coming, Joyce?" Momma asked.

"The tree! It's coming to get me! Nothing else could make such a noise to shake the house!"

I closed my eyes and hid my face in Momma's collar. The low rumbling thunder continued.

I whispered, "Was that the tree again?"

Momma said, "No. God was pushing a wheelbarrow of corn in the heavens."

"He was?" Denny replied.

"Yes," Momma said.

Denny believed her, but I wasn't so sure. I asked, "Then why does God have to make so much noise doing it?"

Momma explained, "It only sounds loud because He's up in the sky over our heads; therefore, pushing a wheel-barrow up there is much noisier than it would be if it were pushed on the ground."

Convinced, I leaned back against Momma and watched as the first large drops of rain hit the windows. Harder and harder it came until the glass was running with water. The drumming of the rain on the glass produced a rhythmical, sleep-inducing sound. Denny was already asleep and I was drowsy so Momma put us both to bed.

As an adult, I seldom hear it rain at night. It has to be a very noisy thunderstorm to wake me up, if I do wake up at all. Now I have no problem going back to sleep while God rolls his corn around the heavens in a wheelbarrow.

A Visit with My Dad

It's five o'clock on a weekday. I hurry to clean the bathroom sink before my dad comes into the house. It's my job to keep it clean, but, with three brothers, it seems that sink is always dirty and it doesn't do me any good to clean it earlier in the day. I finished the sink and walked outdoors to sit on the back step and wait for my dad.

I would have another job when he got home. I always cleaned the paperhanging brushes for him and "worked out" the paintbrushes he had used that day. This day it was three paintbrushes. My dad put them in a can of paint thinner. Slowly I lifted one out and let it drain. Using a stick, I pressed out the excess thinner. Then I took the brush outside to an area on the garage where I "painted" the last of the thinner and paint out of the brush. Then my dad would finish cleaning the brush in fresh brush cleaner. When he was done, he hung the brushes on nails, all in a row, to dry overnight.

While I was working, Daddy took a five gallon bucket and poured two gallons of white paint into it. He then picked up a box containing several tubes of oil paint—red, yellow, blue, and black. I asked Daddy what he was doing.

19

"Well Joyce, Mrs. Tack wants me to paint her kitchen and she wants a very light shade of green, sort of an airy shade, to go with some new curtains she just purchased."

"Do you care if I watch you mix it?"

"Not as long as you don't touch anything."

He carefully added some blue to the white paint. I exclaimed, "I thought you wanted green!"

"Just watch Joyce, to see what happens."

He mixed the blue with a long paint stick. Then he added a lot of yellow.

"It looks sort of sick, Daddy, like how the corn looks in Mrs. Hawk's cornfield."

Daddy added more blue and then he put in a little bit of black. Suddenly the paint turned a deep shade of green. Then he picked up the last bucket of white paint and slowly poured it into the mixture. He stopped from time to time to stir and mix the paint. Very slowly it turned a very delicate shade of green. I was awestruck.

"How did you learn to do that Daddy?"

"I went to school in Memphis, Tennessee, to learn to paint. This was a very important part to learn—how to mix colored paint—because all you can buy is white interior paint."

"Can everyone do this?" I asked.

"Yes, if they understand what colors to mix to get the desired shade."

"Tell me about when you went to school. Did you sit at a desk like I do, with your paints alongside your books? Did the teacher tell you what color to start with? Did—"

"Joyce, I had to work in a laboratory with a teacher who knew everything there is to know about paint, color, types of plaster, wood, and metal. One time I was sent to a beautiful three-story house to varnish the woodwork. I watched the master cabinetmakers use a small tool that cut a sliver of wood and turned it up without breaking it off. They placed a nail in the exposed wood, pounded it in, and then used another tool to counter-sink the nail. Glue was placed over the little strip of exposed wood that held the nail. Carefully they pushed the little piece in place. When they were done, I could not see where the nail was placed. The next day I filed, sanded, and carefully cleaned and varnished this woodwork. It was the most beautiful woodwork I've ever seen."

"Daddy, were you scared to varnish it?"

"No, we were well-schooled in each step to do it. It was part of our training."

"I would have been afraid I would drip some on the floor or smear it on the wall or see a big run!"

"That's why I went to school to learn not to make those mistakes. Want to hear a little story about an experience I had?"

"Yes, yes tell me!"

"When I was in school, the instructor sent three of us to paint some metal pipe in a factory there in Memphis. The two other men took lead paint, but I took aluminum paint, which is made especially for metal.

"The two fellows made much fun of the short red-haired man who brought shiny paint with him. They made smart remarks about how the boss of the plant would fire me for doing such a thing and ruining the 'décor.'

"The pipes were cold when we painted them. Several days later we returned to inspect our work. This time very hot water was running through the pipes. Unfortunately the lead paint was showing signs of blistering and peeling, but the aluminum paint was intact. The other two painting students had forgotten the chapter we'd studied entitled 'Surfaces To Be Painted.' They had to clean the dried paint off those large pipes and repaint them with aluminum paint!"

In wonder I said, "Daddy, when I grow up, I'm not going to be a painter—I'll just let you do it for me."

The High Diving Board

Sometimes our parents drove us to the swimming pool in Pattee Park, and as a family, we would all play in the water. Momma would wear a suit, bathing cap, and bathing sandals, and Daddy would wear swim trunks. Momma never got into the water higher than her waist. She was terrified of water and it must have taken much courage for her to step into the murky water. (You could drop your arms into the water and not see your hands, much less anything lying on the bottom of the pool.) Because she couldn't swim, Momma made sure we children learned to swim. So we were enrolled in the Red Cross swimming lessons, which were held three times a week for several weeks in a row each summer. I was always anxious to show Momma and Daddy how much I had learned in the classes, and how well I could swim.

Access to the five-foot depth and beyond was only gained by swimming across the width of the pool six times. Swimmers could cross twice on their sides, and once upon their backs, but had to swim the remaining three crossings on their stomachs. It was wise to attempt this when first entering the pool. After playing for awhile, sometimes a youngster was too tired to complete the six crossings. One day I felt I was ready to swim the pool six times and earn the privilege to play in the deep water. I made it on the first attempt, although my arms were so tired they were aching by the fifth lap. Yet I was able to force myself to keep going. I just wouldn't give up. The desire I had to play in the deep water was strong motivation.

The next time Momma and Daddy came with us to the pool, I was so proud to show them I could swim in the ten-foot water. I was also getting a little better at diving off the side of the pool. The belly flops didn't happen so often anymore and I could keep my feet together upon entering the water.

My dad asked, "Joyce, have you ever jumped off the diving boards at the deep end?"

My answer was, "No, that's for big kids!"

Daddy said, "I'll give you a quarter to jump off the low board."

I sat on the concrete bench between him and Momma and thought about it. I wasn't sure I was brave enough to do that. I had seen other kids jump off the boards and they seemed to have fun doing it. Eventually I slid off the bench, walked to the tower, and climbed the ladder to the low board. I stood in the small square area facing the board. Some kids were waiting on the ladder so I let them pass me. When no one was waiting, I walked out onto the board, looked down, quickly turned around, and walked back! It took me a few moments to muster my courage before I returned to the end of the board. I wondered, *Is this the way one feels when forced to walk the plank on a pirate ship?* I looked down at the water; it seemed to be much farther away than when I was on the ground looking up. I closed my eyes, took a deep breath, held my nose, and stepped off the end of the board.

For a moment I felt nothing but a falling sensation, then *swoosh* into the water. I threw my arms up and out, up and out, until my head popped out of the water. Quickly, I swam to the ladder to get out, and then walked back to the concrete bench where Momma and Daddy sat to receive their congratulations and encouragement.

After awhile my dad asked, "You going to do that again?"

I said, "Nope. Once was enough."

He said, "I'll give you fifteen cents to do it again."

I sat there figuring, *Five and five is ten, carry one and two is three plus one is four. That's forty cents! That's a lot of money!*

I slipped off the bench and walked back to the diving boards. No one was around them now. I climbed the ladder, stood for a moment on the landing, then walked out to the end of the board. This time I didn't look down. I closed my eyes, took a deep breath, held my nose, and stepped off the board. I thought it really wasn't so bad the second time.

I returned to the bench and sat down. Momma asked, "Was it fun?"

I said, "Well, maybe."

My dad said, "Let's see you jump off the high board."

"Me? Jump off the high board? I'm never going up there, never!" I exclaimed. "I'll get killed up on that board. None of us little girls ever go up there."

Daddy said, "I'll give you a quarter to jump off the high board."

Again, no one said anything. I sat there thinking about the quarter and how sixty-five cents would go a long way toward candy and shows. I wasn't sure I could do it, but finally decided to try. Once again I headed for the tower, started up the ladder, passed the first landing, and stepped onto the high diving board landing. This time I was really afraid. It was a long way down! I was thankful none of my friends were around to see me, because I wanted to go back down the ladder. I don't know how long I stood there, but I finally decided I'd never seen anyone die or even get hurt as a result of jumping off the high board. In fact, most of the time boys would squabble over whose turn it was on the board. I walked to the end of the board and stood there looking out across the pool. I heard someone coming up the ladder and I knew I had to do something before they started yelling at me. I looked down, and no one was in the water beneath me. I took a breath, grabbed my nose, and jumped off the board.

Somehow when I jumped my feet were not quite under me so my bottom made a resounding *smack* when I hit the water. I decided then and there that I'd had enough of that high board! I was so glad to get back to the bench, but the concrete was warm and it increased the stinging on my backside. I jumped off the bench and quickly slid into the water in front of Daddy and Momma. I stayed there until the burning stopped.

Daddy said, "Remember, Joyce, to take your time before entering the water. Wait until you're ready and then jump. I'll give you fifteen cents to try it again."

This time I waited until the boys playing on the high board had moved to the springboard before I went back. When I walked out on the high board, I remembered Daddy's advice and took my time before stepping off the end. I had no problems entering the water, although I noticed it took a little longer to stop my descent in the water from the high board! This was a little scary because the deep water was so dark, but, all things considered, I decided jumping off of diving boards was an easy way to earn money. Unfortunately, my dad didn't offer me any more. But then, he didn't need to, because I no longer feared "going off" the high diving boards!

Warm Summer Rains

Growing up, my family lived at 1624 North Street, on the corner of Seventh. Beyond our house North Street ended in a gravel road. But from Sixth Street to Fifth Street, North Street was paved and sloped slightly. Because there must not have been an intake close by, rainwater would always puddle at the intersection of Fifth Street, and took a long time to drain away. Thus, many of the neighborhood children would run down there to play during a warm summer rain. Some of the bigger boys in the neighborhood (potential engineers, I suppose) would dam up the water on its way to the intersection to form small pools. Denny and I would take pieces of wood to these pools and pretend they were our boats. We would see whose boat could float the farthest before becoming grounded. If a boat got stuck, we could use a small tree branch to dislodge it without destroying the dam.

When a rain stopped, the flow of water slowed so boats would no longer float. Then Denny and I would play in the intersection where the water was deep enough to come up to our knees. We would take turns marching around kicking the water and trying to run through it. (I think we two were the first in the neighborhood to introduce walking in water.) We always tried to be careful and not get the muddy water all over us, but never with much success. When we were tired of playing in the water, we would return home.

One day the sun came out as we headed home, and to my surprise and delight, a rainbow came down right into our front yard! Upon seeing the rainbow, Denny and I immediately set out looking for the pot of gold.

After searching frantically for a few minutes, I said, "I don't understand! Everyone says there's a pot of gold sitting right there at the end of a rainbow for all to see. And it's there in every picture I've ever seen."

Denny said, "Where'd it go? Who do you think took it?"

I said, "No one could've taken it because we're the only ones around."

We were both disappointed, and decided since there was no gold, the story must be another myth like the one about Santa Claus. But our disappointment was quickly dispersed by our fascination with the rainbow. Cautiously, we put our hands into the bright colors, then swished them back and forth. The rainbow felt damp like a mist. We walked through it, we ran through it, and then we danced through it. In and out, around and around we went through this beautiful shaft of incredible color that was reaching down from the sky into our front yard. Our enchantment with this rainbow was short-lived, though. It did not linger as one in the sky usually does, but slowly faded away, then was gone. It vanished as quickly as our belief in the pot of gold.

Only the week before, my Sunday school teacher Mrs. Snipe had taught us about how God placed the rainbow in the sky as a reminder of His promise to never destroy the earth again with water. I wonder if He heard our laughter as we played in His rainbow that day.

Me and Dorothy

I had a friend named Dorothy Meier who lived on a farm east of Perry. Beaver Creek ran through the farm, and many, many hours were wiled away playing with Dorothy "down at the crick." We would fish, catch turtles, throw rocks into the water, sink our feet and legs into the cold mud, or just jump into the water seeing who could make the biggest splash to scare away any fish or turtles or snakes that might be waiting to bite us.

Dorothy's father had a watermelon patch on the other side of the creek. One day we decided to go pick the ripe melons we had heard her parents talking about the night before. We took Dorothy's wagon to the top of the drive-way leading to the pasture, gave the wagon a push, and jumped in for the short ride down the hill. We took turns riding in and pulling the wagon until we got to the creek. There was one shallow place close to a plank footbridge where we could easily pull the wagon through the water and up the bank to the other side. Being barefoot, we had to be careful not to step on any sand burs, which were all too plentiful on that side of the creek. From there, we went past a cabin, which was occupied by Hank Aleck, a very, very old man. We thought he had to be forty-five, maybe even fifty years old, and would surely die any day because he was so old. (We had to steer clear of him because the day before we had locked him in his cabin!)

When we arrived at the patch, we saw many ripe melons just waiting to be harvested. Carefully we went around and thumped each one to determine which were really ready to be eaten. We chose five of the largest melons and between the two of us managed to get them into the wagon. Now with our heavy load, one of us had to pull while the other pushed. It was a real effort to get the wagon back as far as the creek, for often the wheels would sink into the soft, sandy soil requiring us both to stop and lift it a little. We pulled the wagon through the water onto the sandbar where we became completely bogged down in the sand. We sat on the bridge dangling our feet in the water contemplating our problem and what we were going to do about it. We decided that since we had slipped out of the house that morning without any breakfast, we would just eat one of the melons.

We rolled one off the wagon into the sand and onto the footbridge. We sat straddling the bridge with the melon between us and dipped water with our hands to wash off the sand and dirt. Together we picked up the melon and smacked it sharply on the plank. It burst open between us, one half falling into the water. But there was something very much wrong. Instead of its insides being red and juicy, it was pale and sickly pink looking. In all my nine years I'd not seen such a melon! We could not let it be known that we had made a big mistake, so I went to retrieve the half that was slowly drifting downstream. We dug a hole in the sand with our hands and buried the green melon, thinking, *Out of sight, out of mind.*

We returned to the wagon, chose another melon, rolled it through the sand onto the bridge, and resumed our seats on either side of it. Once again we washed it before we cracked it open. To our great surprise, its insides were also as green as they could be! Therefore, another sand burial took place. We stood by the wagon looking down upon the three remaining melons and decided to break them open on the side of the wagon to save ourselves all the work of getting them to the bridge. Obviously, our self-confidence in melon choosing was not what it had been an hour before. To our dismay, the last three were no riper than the first two! It took us a little longer to bury the last of them. But we had to work fast before Dorothy's mother or father discovered what we had done with the five largest melons in their patch! The rest of the day went well—no more mischief for us—and we were so good that Dorothy's mother thought we were sick and made us lay down in the afternoon.

The next morning we got up, quickly dressed, and slipped down the stairs planning to head to the creek to play. Our plans came to an abrupt halt upon seeing both her parents seated at the kitchen table waiting for us, and they weren't smiling. It occurred to me that we were probably in trouble. We washed our hands and faces at the sink and started for the table. I knew for sure that Dorothy thought we were in trouble when she slipped around on the other side of her father to sit, leaving me next to her mother. This left me more than a little wary.

Her mother asked, "Were you girls over to Hank's cabin the other day?"

Oh boy! Old Hank had been over and told on us and there I sat within easy reach of the long arm of the law! The hair started crawling on the back of my neck.

"Joyce?"

"Yes, Ma'am, me 'n Dorothy, we was over there." I could hardly speak because I thought sure she would swat me one.

"Did you turn the outside lock on Hank's door?"

"No, Ma'am." *I* really hadn't done it. I'd hid in a hollow watching as Dorothy snuck up and turned the lock. Both of us watched as Hank tried to open his door. After a while we walked up to the cabin singing and laughing and knocked on his door. He asked us to let him out and we did. We told him we'd seen the Tingwald boys around the cabin. He was sure mad and I don't think he believed the story about the Tingwald boys.

"Dorothy," said her mother, "you turned the lock on Hank's door?"

Dorothy answered, "Just a little bit. He could of shook the door and got out."

Dorothy's mother started sputtering half in German and half in English. "You girls are getting into too much trouble. You—"

"Now, now, Mother," interrupted Dorothy's father, "they be little girls and they didn't hurt anyone."

"Another thing," her mother said, "what did you do with the watermelons you picked from the patch?"

I looked at Dorothy and wondered, *How did they know about the melons?* Had Hank seen us? I hadn't seen him around anywhere yesterday. Surely he wouldn't have told

36

on us if he did see us. But maybe he did. He was pretty steamed about us locking him in the cabin, even after we let him out! Dorothy quickly looked at her father, not wishing to look her mother in the eye. I'm sure she was glad she was sitting out of her mother's reach.

Her father calmly spoke, "You girls must not play around the creek today. It came up quite high last night— must have had a big rain north of here." I thought, *So that's why they were waiting for us, to keep us from going to the crick to play. But how did her mother know about the melons?*

"Also," her father continued, "when the melons are ready I will take you with the team and wagon to get them. Those you buried in the sand yesterday were washed out by the rising water this morning."

So Mother Nature had been the one to expose our secret of the day before! That day I learned that no matter how hard you try to cover up something, sooner or later it will surface.

"The circus is coming, the circus is coming!" I cried as I entered the front door. "Momma, Momma, Denny, the circus is coming to town and they are going to unload the animals at half past five tomorrow morning! Can we go Momma, can we, huh?"

Momma said, "Joyce, slow down a bit. Yes, I know it's coming."

"Can we go see the animals Momma?" I asked.

"Please, please, please!" said Denny.

"Joyce, Dennis, quiet down. You are talking entirely too fast and too loud. When your father comes home we will discuss this more."

Denny said, "I saw a picture of a lion with his mouth open, and he had big teeth and John said, 'Two bites from him and you'd be all gone!'"

"Oh, Denny. The lions are in cages and can't get out. And they won't let little kids like us near the cage," I said.

"Who told you that?" he asked.

"The big kids down on Fifth Street. They are in the eighth grade and know everything. Just ask them. They'll tell you."

Anxiously we waited for Daddy to come home. About 5:30 PM he appeared. He took care of his paperhanging equipment as usual, handed me the paper brushes to wash, and the meat for supper to give to Momma. He didn't seem excited at all! He never said a word about the circus coming to town and I wondered if he had heard about it. I hurried to the house, gave Momma the meat, and went into the garage to clean the brushes.

We all assembled at the supper table, hands folded in our laps, patiently waiting for the blessing to be said. Daddy chose to give it himself tonight. He was thankful for the food. (I was thankful that the meat wasn't liver!)

As soon as Daddy finished John asked, "Did you hear the circus is coming to town?"

Daddy answered, "Yes, I heard. This is a big one; it'll have three rings. There will be a parade downtown in the morning before the afternoon performance."

"Can we go Daddy?" I asked.

"Yes, we'll all go and then come home for dinner. I have to go back to work, but you children may attend the afternoon show."

My heart jumped. Denny hollered, "I get to go! I get to go! I get to go!"

The next morning as we all piled into Daddy's pickup, I could hardly contain myself. I never thought we would ever reach downtown!

Second Street was lined with cars and people everywhere. Denny and I scrambled out of the pickup onto the street, pushed our way to the curb, and sat down. The parade began with the elephants. A woman dressed in fancy clothes sat on the first elephant's back. There were horses with long white manes with women and men all dressed in colorful finery riding them. Then came the tigers in their cages. One was pacing back and forth, but the others were lying down with their eyes closed like they were sleeping. They didn't fool me; their tails were flipping just like our kitty, Miss Ritzey flips her tail when she's awake but laying down. Next a very long car with several rows of seats came by. There were only three occupants in the car. The driver sat in the front seat and a fat woman and another heavy man sat in the back seat. All of a sudden the front end of the car went up in the air and the car continued down the street on its back two wheels! The two people in the back seat leaned forward and the car came down on four wheels and drove on past us. Wow! I'd never seen anything like that! The parade passed all too quickly. Then it was time to go home.

The circus was to be at the old fairgrounds south of Perry. After dinner, Momma gave each of us a nickel to get in the gate. John and George took off on a run to join their friends. Denny and I started out and joined some of the neighbor kids: little Gene Hurd, Don and LaVonne McDivitt, and Dorothy Hawk. Quite a few more joined us on the long walk to the fairgrounds. I think every kid in town was there. Several were carrying popcorn in grocery sacks to eat during the show. All were happily talking about what they had seen in the parade, and bubbling over with antic- ipation of the tent show.

We arrived at the front of the big tent where the tick- ets were sold. We bought our tickets and then walked sin- gle file into the tent. Inside a man took our tickets and told us where to go. Kids with five-cent tickets were sent to the far end of the three rings to sit on the ground. Those who paid more got to sit in the bleachers where they could view all three rings from the side. My friend Dorothy Meier sat in the bleachers with her mother. She motioned for me to join them, but I only had the five-cent ticket so had to move on. Denny and I sat on the ground as near to the front as we could get. The kids who brought sacks of popcorn opened them up and shared with all the kids there. What a treat!

The trumpet sounded and the circus began. The elephants came thundering in, shaking the ground beneath us. Pretty ladies were riding on their backs and sitting on their heads. One even sat on an elephant's trunk! They were followed by horses with ribbons and flowers on their halters. A woman was standing up while riding the lead horse. Calliope music filled the air while a man wearing tights and no shirt was walking on a wire stretched across the ring in front of us. The ringmaster stood in the middle ring wearing a black suit with tails, a bow tie, a top hat, and white gloves. He carried a fancy sparkle-covered bullhorn, and used it to call our attention to the trapeze artists who were swinging in the air high above the three rings.

Then the clowns came in doing handsprings, somersaults, and walking on their hands. They came very close to where we were sitting. One clown wore a barrel for his clothes. Denny and I laughed so hard at him our sides hurt. Another clown juggled three, four, and then five balls in the air. He threw them so high I thought he would lose them! Not once did he miss. A man on stilts with long black pants and a high top hat strolled past us, tipping his hat to us. (But this man didn't have anything on Don Mc-Divitt, who owned a pair of stilts with overalls over them that had extended legs. Don's stilts were so tall he had to go to his front porch and stand on the railing just to get on them!) Then the bears came rolling and tumbling along into the ring in front of us. As they were leaving, little dogs came in and climbed ladders and one sat in a swing watching the other animals.

By the time the performance was over, we were so excited with all we had seen, the long walk home didn't bother us. My brothers and I and our friends talked for days about the circus.

Making Cider Vinegar

One summer afternoon our dad drove into the yard with something very large in his truck box. Quickly I stopped playing on the swing and ran to see what he had. It was a press used to squeeze liquid from lard or apples. He had borrowed it from some friends who lived in the country.

"George, John," he called, as he unloaded his ladders and paint buckets and carried them into the garage.

"Joyce, go tell the boys I need them to help me unload this apple press, and then you come back. There are some paintbrushes for you to work out for me."

I ran into the house and found George, John, and Denny listening to *Jack Armstrong, the All-American Boy* on the radio.

"George! John! Daddy needs you to help him unload a great big apple press. Right away!"

The boys jumped up from the living room floor, and the three of us scampered outdoors to the back driveway. Denny had trouble keeping up, but managed to get outdoors with the rest of us. Dad had moved the pickup into the garage and had pulled the press to the back edge of the truck box. The three of them then lifted the press off the truck and carefully placed it on the table which was standing in the garage. After watching all this I went to work cleaning the paintbrushes for my dad.

At the supper table, Daddy told us what he planned to do with the apple press.

"Tomorrow morning," he said, "we will drive out to Mr. J. L. Blake's to pick up apples from a tree in his timber." (The Blakes were farmers who lived about four miles northeast of Perry. I think the previous fall the boys may have picked up walnuts from this same farm.)

The next morning Daddy and the boys moved the press outdoors so Momma could clean it while we were gone. I was excited because I could go help pick up apples. As soon as breakfast was over, I think I may have been first into the pickup, anxious to get started. George and John were not in such a hurry, and did not share the excitement with me. (I would soon learn that picking up apples was more work than fun.)

It didn't take long to drive the few miles to the Blake residence. While my dad was talking to Mr. Blake, Mrs. Blake took me to her garden to show me all her pretty flowers. At this time of year there were many different colored phlox in bloom. Mrs. Blake was such a pleasant person; I liked her. She was a soft-spoken old-fashioned lady wearing a rather long cotton dress with an apron over it. I would have liked to have spent more time with her, but I heard the pickup start and I sure didn't want to miss the trip to the timber to pick up apples.

Hurriedly, I got into the truck box with George and John. Slowly we drove to the pasture and the boys jumped out to open the gate for the pickup to pass through, and then quickly closed and latched it so the cows couldn't get out. Through the pasture and into the timber we drove. It became a little hilly in the timber, but soon we found the apple tree, and it was really loaded. Even the ground was covered!

"Now Joyce," said my dad, "be sure you do not pick up any rotten or wormy ones. Wormy apples will have a little hole or sometimes just a little brown dot on them. They are no good and we can't use them."

I grabbed a bucket and started to fill it with apples. I took the time to look each one over good, not wishing to save a bad one. I was bent over my bucket when *Wham!* my backside was smacked with an apple. I turned around but could not tell which of my brothers was the good shot, as they were both very busy with their heads down. I was careful not to present such a tempting target for them again!

It didn't take us long to fill the pickup with these large, juicy, and sweet-to-the-taste apples. We all climbed aboard, stepping on and crawling over one another, crowding into the front seat. Amid yips and yells we headed for the open pasture. It was nice going until we came to the first small hill. The pickup could not make it to the top of the small incline. The wheels were spinning on the damp grass; the load was just too much for the little pickup.

"Hey you kids," my dad shouted. "Get out and push me up the hill!"

We all bailed out and started pushing for all we were worth. The wheels spun just a little on the grass but took hold and up we went to the top. We thought our dad would stop and let us back on. Instead he kept going, taking a run for each of the small hills left. We hollered, yelled, and ran after him, thinking he would leave us to walk all the way back, but he waited for us at the edge of the cleared pasture. The distance wasn't far so we ran most of the way. We got into the pickup again and started for the gate. John and George hopped out to open and close the gate and we were on our way home. I must admit I was a little tired, but still excited!

Daddy eased the pickup into the back driveway past the press and a little onto the back walk. The press was made of oak wood and it gleamed almost white from Momma's scrub brush. Before it could be used, however, we needed to wash the apples. George and John hauled them a bucket at a time to the pump at the well. The apple washing started and continued until all the apples were clean. Momma and Daddy quartered the apples, looking for worms, and then dumped them into the press a bucket full at a time. Daddy turned the handle on the press and soon the juice was pouring out a little spout at the bottom. Momma caught it in gallon jugs she had washed and sterilized. We worked most of the afternoon washing and pressing our apples. The skins, seeds, and apple residue were taken by the bucket full and fed to our chickens and hogs. (Nothing edible ever went to waste during the Depression.)

There must have been six or seven gallon jugs full of juice and the remainder was in two-quart jars. The jars were taken to the house for us to drink and enjoy. While Daddy was cleaning up the press to return it, Momma was cutting a small piece of "mother" to place in each gallon jug to make the juice more readily turn into vinegar. ("Mother" was a thick piece of jelly-like substance that formed in the bottom of vinegar bottles. I haven't seen any of it since processed vinegar became available.) I then

48

helped Momma cut squares of cheesecloth, folding each piece several times and then tying it tightly over the mouth of each jug. The cheesecloth kept bugs out of the vinegar while it sat in the sun curing. About four days after it had been sitting in the sun, I opened one jug to see if it was still sweet. To my disappointment it was almost pure vinegar!

Soon after, Momma sealed the jugs. She used the cider vinegar for canning and table use. Almost every day we had sliced cucumbers and onions on the table. Momma made sweet pickles, dill pickles, bread and butter pickles, and relish from our garden produce, using the vinegar we had made earlier in the summer. All winter long we enjoyed the fruit of our summer labor.

Now when I want vinegar, relish, or pickles, I choose them from a large variety on display at the grocery store. Times have changed since I was a child so long ago—and so has the taste of the pickles and relish I now use!

A Very Hot Summer

The summer of 1936 was hot and dry. Even the breeze, if there was any, would burn your face and neck with its heat. Momma and most of the neighborhood women would get up very early in the morning to do their work because by noon the heat was often unbearable.

One Sunday morning we left earlier than usual to attend Sunday school and church. The air was still, the sky was clear, and the sun was shining intensely. We knew we were in for another "scorcher." I wore my "Sunday best", which was a sleeveless cotton print dress, not to be worn for everyday or to school. My shoes were black patent and my hose were white cotton anklets. We all walked out to the garage to get into the 1929 Model A Ford pickup. Because Daddy used this truck for his painting and wallpapering business, on Saturday evenings he always removed all the canvas drop cloths, paint cans, and ladders, so we could all get into it comfortably. I always sat between Daddy and Momma in the front seat and the boys sat in the truck box. I kept my knees and legs close to Momma because the gear shift came up almost to the seat, and Daddy would sternly remind me to get my legs and knees over. Daddy always parked in the shade under a tree so it wouldn't be so terribly hot for the boys to sit in the metal truck box to return home.

That day we arrived at the old Methodist Church in plenty of time to visit with friends and to find a seat. Some of the girls in my class were Juanita Tolle Dorman, Francis Thomas, Virginia Gray, Ethel Anfinson, Benita Cornelous, and Louretta Haynes. We went to the gym where wooden folding chairs were set up for us children to sit on. Mrs. Meelick, a devoted church worker, often opened the little service for us. We would sing a song from the hymnal. Many times it was the "Books of the Bible" song. (At that time, singing this song was one of the popular methods of teaching children the books in order.) One time when Mrs. Meelick was speaking to us, she offered fifty cents to any child who could recite the Ten Commandments. Unfortunately, she didn't have any takers. Several of us studied to learn them, but she never offered again. I must admit her strategy did have results!

After the opening song, we were dismissed to go to our classrooms, which were located along the two walls of the gym. Dividers on wheels separated the classes. Thus, each room had three sides with the fourth being open to the gym. Our Sunday school teacher always had interesting stories to tell us about the early characters in the Bible. We loved them and would listen spellbound to her stories of Noah and the great flood, baby Moses, King David, and a person named Jonah who didn't want to do God's bidding, so ended up in the belly of a whale. The telling of those stories kept us coming back week after week, and we learned much from God's instruction book.

Because we hadn't found any shade to park under, when church was over that day the truck box was very hot. So Denny got to sit in the cab on Momma's lap. Because he was tall for his age, his feet touched the floor. He was crowding me and I didn't like it, but thought better of expressing my discomfort. Daddy let George and John stand on the running boards on the sides of the truck. They hung onto the bars that contained the snaps for the heavy window curtains.

After church, Momma usually prepared a big Sunday dinner for us, even in hot weather, because Sundays were always special. As this particular afternoon drew on, it became unbearably hot. The breeze coming in our south windows in the living room felt like your face and arms were being seared. Daddy shut the windows. It was actually cooler in the house without the windows open!

Daddy sent me to the well to fill the aluminum water pitcher. I was to pump two pitchers full and dump them into a barrel sitting close to the pump. This water was used to water the chickens. The third pitcher was really cold and showed heavy condensation on the outside. I hurried it to the house and we all had a cold drink of sweet well water. I can still feel the coolness of it as it slipped down my throat leaving me refreshed. I was sent out again before supper to get another pitcherful. This time it was used to dilute tea. Momma chipped ice from the block in the icebox and added it just before she poured the tea in our glasses. When she poured tea, sometimes little chips of ice would slip under the lip guard on the pitcher into our glasses. What a treat!

When the sun became low in the sky, the breeze didn't seem so hot. Momma and Daddy pulled the wicker rockers outdoors into the yard. A blanket was spread on the ground for us children to sit on. As it became dark, we watched for shooting stars, and tried to make wishes before one went out. We would say, "I wish I may, I wish I might, have the wish I wish tonight." Sometimes I wished for candy, or to go out to Midgie Wilson's, or out to Dorothy Meier's to play in Beaver Creek, and sometimes I wished for ice cream. If I received any of those wishes, I didn't connect them to a shooting star, because the wish had long been forgotten.

As we laid on our backs watching for shooting stars, we became drowsy. I thought, *How nice it would be to just sleep here in the coolness of the evening!* But, that never happened because when we became quiet, Momma knew we were sleepy and made us get up to go to bed. I got into my night clothes, and just flopped onto my bed. I knew nothing until morning. How sweet the sleep was.

Fall

Going Back to School

The last few weeks of August were always an exciting time of preparation at our house. School began the day after Labor Day, so Momma would take us to Webster School to register. (There were three elementary schools in Perry—Webster, Roosevelt, and Lincoln. Webster was the school closest to our house on Seventh and North Streets.) We would each get a list of the books needed for the year. Momma would go over our lists and mark the books we would have to purchase. Then Daddy would take us downtown to Ainley's Bookstore (on Willis Avenue next to Ray B. Smith's drugstore) to buy our books.

Most of the time Denny and I didn't get new books, but received hand-me-downs from George and John. But, we were always allowed to choose new pencils, tablets, pens, pen points, and ink. And sometimes, if we needed them, new rulers, paints, and erasers. One year George and John got a compass and a protractor. How I envied them! They let Denny and me play with these items. We had fun drawing circles and arcs on wallpaper samples from a book Daddy had given us to play with. We often colored these drawings and thought they were pretty—Momma always told us they were!

The start of a new year also required new shoes and usually, new clothes. Each fall, Momma would take me downtown to Dennis Graney's shoe store (on Second Street across from the library) to buy a new pair of brown lace Oxfords. Momma made sure they fit me, yet had plenty of room left over for my toes to grow. I never remember outgrowing a pair of shoes; I always wore them out.

One fall, I saw some dresses in J.C. Penney's catalog that I liked. Momma carefully studied each picture and then made patterns for the dresses. Then she took me downtown to Ringham's Dry Goods Store (on Second Street), where she chose five lengths of cotton prints similar to the colors shown in the catalog. When Momma was done sewing, I had five Penney look-alike dresses to wear.

I always anticipated the first day of school—a new teacher, a different room, and a reunion with classmates I hadn't seen all summer. There was much comparing and catching up to do. The swings, teeter-totters, and merry-go-rounds all had new coats of paint, and stood waiting for us to play on them. Our classroom floor was newly varnished so it squeaked when we walked on it. George Washington was still hanging on the wall, and the U.S. flag stood in the corner of the room. (We would stand every day after roll call and face it to give the Pledge of Allegiance.) Seat assignments were given this first day as well. I liked sitting at the front of the classroom, and often did because my last name started with an "A."

One of my favorite teachers was Miss Cunningham, who came to our classroom once a week for Art. She encouraged us to make objects out of colored construction paper, and helped us make pencil drawings. Miss Cunningham also instructed us in Penmanship, helping us practice our "ovals" and "push-pulls" to become legible writers. (I never did learn to use my whole arm as she advocated; hence, my writing to this day is not as smooth as the Palmer Method examples that were displayed above the blackboard.)

It was fun helping the teachers. They used to let the students take turns ringing the bell for school to begin and for recess to conclude. At the end of the day, one student from each class was allowed to erase the blackboard and take the erasers outdoors to pound out the dust. This was a big treat! On the weekend, Mr. Callahan (the custodian) would wipe the blackboards and the eraser troughs with a damp cloth. How nice the blackboards looked on Monday morning to start the new week.

School wasn't without its rules. Those of us who went home for lunch were not allowed to be on the school grounds before ten minutes of one during lunch hours. So we would congregate on the corner of Fourth and North Streets until someone yelled it was time, and then the stampede was on to get to the playground. Most of the time we were disappointed; the playground equipment was fully occupied by students who ate lunch at school.

Before being dismissed each day, we would put away our books in our desks, and sit with folded hands. Sometimes we would line up at the door so the teacher could lead us down the hall, up or down the stairs, and then out the front door. We were quiet and orderly until we stepped over the threshold. Then we could laugh and talk to one another and be playful children again.

Going back to school had its drawbacks. Even though hot days in September and October were common, the

Pattee Pool closed every year on Labor Day. (Dewayne Lewiston eventually changed that for Perry youngsters when he was mayor. He probably remembered the days when school was dismissed because of the heat, and we had no place to go swimming!)

Quilt Making

Late one afternoon in early September, we children were playing outside when Daddy pulled into the driveway. He leaned out the window of his 1929 Model A Ford pickup and called,

"George, John, I need your help."

As Daddy drove around to the garage, I noticed something fluttering up and down inside the truck bed. *What could that be,* I wondered. Not wishing to miss anything, I ran along to see.

Daddy parked the truck and I stepped up on one of the running boards. Inside the truck box were three baskets full of wool samples, as well as a pile of large books.

"Where did you get these, Daddy?" I asked.

He said, "Jean McCammon decided to clean out his stock room. He gave them to me." (Jean McCammon owned a clothing store in downtown Perry.)

I ran behind George and John as they carried the baskets and books to our enclosed front porch. The storm windows were still in place, and I felt the warm sun pouring in through the glass as Denny and I sat on the floor between the baskets to look at the samples. There were several solids in gray, blue, black, and tan, as well as many pinstripe and checked pieces in various colors.

"Look Denny!" I said, holding up a bright red square.

Quickly turning over more pieces, we found another red square and then another.

"There's a whole bunch of them!" he shouted.

The front door opened and Momma came out to the porch to peek at what we were doing.

At the bottom of one of the baskets, I discovered some lovely cream-colored squares.

"What are we going to do with all these pieces of wool?" I asked.

Momma answered, "We are going to make quilts for the beds."

I looked at her. "Oh Momma, please may I have all these red and cream ones in mine?"

Momma replied, "Joyce, don't you think it would be nice to share them so all five of the quilts will be pretty?"

Denny shouted, "Yeah, don't be a big fat pig, Joyce!"

"But, but, Momma why—"

Denny interrupted me. "Oink, oink, oink!"

I turned to him. "You better quit, Denny, before I smack you one!"

Momma said, "That's enough you two. I don't want to hear anymore from either of you."

"Yes, Momma," I answered, not wanting her to get a switch from the lilac bush to help us remember we were not to argue with one another.

However, when Momma bent over one of the baskets, I looked at Denny cross-eyed, so he stuck his tongue out at me!

After supper, Momma opened the dining room table and put in all three of its leaves. Then she and George emptied the baskets and started sorting the wool pieces by color, pattern, and size. Meanwhile, Denny and I joined John on the front porch where he was tearing more samples from inside the books.

"Be careful not to stretch the fabric when you remove it," he said, "and also don't leave a long strip of paper on the back."

Even with all of us working together, the wool samples kept us busy until late in the evening. Before he went to bed, John carried the empty books to the burn barrel in the garden.

The next morning I asked, "Momma, when will you start making the quilts?"

"Today," she replied.

"Momma?"

"Yes Joyce?"

I looked longingly at the piles of red pieces. "Will you work on my quilt first?"

Momma smiled. "No. I think the first one should go to George, as he's the oldest."

Unfortunately, I couldn't dispute that point.

That afternoon Momma carefully cut the selected pieces into equally sized squares, then pinned the squares together into long strips. After supper, Daddy helped her move the treadle sewing machine closer to the table so she could begin sewing.

Over the next week, Momma worked on George's quilt whenever she could. The sewing was tedious, as she had to pull out each pin as she came to it, rather than risk breaking the needle on the machine. After she sewed together the squares in each strip, Momma took the strips to the ironing board, where she gently pressed open all the seams. Once she'd pressed all the strips, Momma laid them side by side lengthwise on the table and asked George to help her pin them together. It was so exciting to watch a quilt emerge as they worked! Momma sewed the strips together and gave them each a final press. At last, she had a top large enough for a double bed.

"Momma, will you work on John's next?" I asked, fingering a red square in the beautiful quilt.

"Yes, Joyce, but we have to finish George's first."

That weekend Momma and Daddy went downtown and bought rolls of wool batting, skeins of yarn, and yards of striped blue flannel to back the quilts. Momma laid the flannel on the table, and unrolled the batting over it. Then she unfolded the rows of colorful squares and laid them on top.

George helped Momma finish his quilt. Carefully, they sewed together the three layers around the edges. When they had finished, Momma laid the skeins of yarn on the table.

She asked, "George, what color would you like the ties to be?"

His choices were: blue, green, red, purple, and yellow. Immediately, I knew which color I wanted.

"I'll take blue," he said.

I was so relieved! I didn't want blue yarn for my quilt.

Denny and I watched as Momma showed George how to cut the blue yarn into small pieces, poke them through at the corners of each square, and then tie them into knots.

This took a few more days to complete. Finally, one night after supper, we all gathered around the dining room table and Momma displayed the finished quilt. We were all proud of it. When we were through admiring it, Momma carefully folded the quilt.

"Aren't you going to put it on George's bed?" I asked her.

She smiled. "Not yet. I'm going to put it in the closet in the east bedroom until cold weather comes."

"Are you going to work on my quilt next?" I asked.

"No Joyce," she said. "Tomorrow I'll begin working on John's quilt."

Over the next week, John helped Momma assemble his quilt. When it came time for him to choose his yarn, Momma laid the green, yellow, red, and purple rolls on the table. "What color would you like your ties to be, John?" she asked.

I held my breath.

John thought for a moment. "Green, I suppose."

I exhaled. I thought, *I'll get my color after all!*

Momma showed John how to cut and tie the yarn. When the quilt was finished, we all gathered around to admire it. This time when Momma folded John's quilt, I knew where she was taking it.

When she came downstairs, Momma said, "Joyce, your quilt is next."

"Do I get to help you make my quilt, Momma?" I asked.

Momma smiled. "I think I'll have George help me put it together, but you may help me tie it."

I clapped my hands. "Oh goodie! And Momma, I want the red yarn!"

After making and storing my beautiful quilt, Momma asked George to help make and tie Denny's as well. Denny chose the yellow yarn.

Because it was a bigger bed, Momma and Daddy's quilt needed more strips, although by that time there weren't many squares of fabric left. Nevertheless, their quilt turned out beautifully with its purple ties. I watched as Momma carefully folded her quilt and placed it with the others.

One night in mid-October, the weather turned cold. Momma took we children upstairs to the east room's closet one at a time to get our quilts. During warm weather, we had what were known as "double sheet blankets" on our beds. (These were not two separate sheets, but actually one long piece of flannel folded in half.) Momma helped each of us place our quilts between the halves of our sheet blankets in order to keep them clean. I was so proud that night as I climbed under my beautiful quilt with its bright red yarn that I'd helped tie. I felt warm and snug that night and many more nights thereafter.

A Harvest Time Treat

Early one Saturday morning in late September, I heard my dad call,

"George! John! Time to get up!"

Now, why would Daddy be calling the boys at this hour? I wondered. Not wanting to miss anything, I jumped out of bed and ran to the stairwell to see what was going on.

I met John coming from his room and asked him, "Why are you getting up so early?"

He said, "Oh, Daddy wants us to pick the popcorn before we go to work. He said it was dry enough to pop now, and he's afraid it will be rained on if we don't get it out of the field."

Wow, I thought. *Fresh popcorn! We just used up what was left of last year's corn. If I tag along with them, maybe Daddy will let me help.*

(He and Momma hadn't let me help hull walnuts because they said my hands would get stained. The boys at school would compare their walnut-stained hands to see whose was darkest. Most boys would rub their hands with stain before they left for school. George and John were no different!)

67

Quickly, I dressed and ran to the bathroom to wash my face and hands and to comb my hair. (This was a rule that Momma and Daddy insisted we all observe: when you come to the table you are to be washed and combed. Denny was always being sent back to re-wash his hands and to get rid of the "high water mark" on his wrists and on his face. Even I was sent back a time or two to do a better job!)

I walked into the kitchen. "Morning Daddy, Morning Momma! Oh goodie! I see you have French toast. I sure like it better than pancakes."

Denny was almost finished eating. He was an early riser, so usually beat the rest of us children to the table each morning. He and I could only get around one slice of French toast apiece, but George and John could each eat five or six pieces. Once Daddy said that John had a hollow leg. I thought about this for a minute. *His leg looks like mine…I wonder how it got hollow?*

I asked Momma and she said, "It's just an expression, Joyce, meaning John eats so much he must be putting all that food into a hollow leg."

Grown-ups sure do know a lot of things, I thought.

When everyone was finished eating, Daddy, George, and John, went to the garage to get gunnysacks to hold the corn. I followed them up to the corn patch. I was afraid Daddy would send me back to the house, but he didn't. Daddy took two rows, and George and John each took one row, shucking the popcorn as they picked it. Because the corn stalks were dry, the black and yellow spiders were quite visible. The big kids said if they bite you, you die right on the spot. Not wanting to drop dead, I found a row where there were no spiders, and picked an ear.

I tried to shuck it in one motion like Daddy and my brothers did, but the corn slipped through my hands. By the time I'd shucked one ear of corn (by pulling back the husks one at a time), Daddy and my brothers were way ahead of me. *I'm not much help,* I thought. *Guess I'm too little for the job...I'm going back to the house.* About an hour later, Daddy and the boys were finished picking corn. They hung the bags from four long wires attached to the rafters in the garage. (This way the corn could dry and not become rancid. And mice could not climb down the wires so the corn was always clean.)

Making popcorn was a special treat. One of us children would go out to the garage, take down a bag, and remove some ears. Momma would place her dishpan on a stool outdoors and we children would stand around it and help shell the corn. Afterwards, Momma would take her colander and pour the shelled corn into it. Then she began a process she called "fanning." She would pour the corn back and forth so the little husks flew away in the breeze, leaving the clean kernels ready to be popped. If the corn was too dry to pop, Momma would run water into the colander and rinse it. Then she would dump the wet corn onto a clean dishtowel where she would roll and rub it until all the water was gone.

One time John asked, "What makes a kernel of corn pop?"

Momma answered, "When corn is heated, the moisture inside a kernel turns to steam, causing it to swell. When the pressure is great enough the kernel will split open and the insides will puff out fluffy."

Momma didn't have a store-bought popcorn popper, but used a kettle with a round lid on it. (Every family I knew had at least one of these kettles and used them to boil potatoes, cook sweet corn, and can tomatoes and peaches. It was an essential piece of equipment in the kitchen.)

Sometimes for a real harvest treat, Momma would make popcorn balls. All I was allowed to do was carry the sorghum to the table. George, John, and Momma did the rest. Denny and I sat on Daddy's chair at the end of the table, out of the way, watching as they measured the sugar, water, and sorghum to make the syrup, and popped the corn. George and John separated the popcorn from the "old maids." ("Old maids" were kernels that didn't pop.) These were dumped into a bowl and placed in front of Denny and me to eat. When all was ready, Momma gave George a wooden spoon to stir the popcorn as she poured the syrup over it. Denny and I remained silent and still because this was a very touchy job—one slip and someone could get burned with the hot syrup. Momma finished pouring and took over the stirring. George and John buttered their hands to keep the syrup from sticking as they formed the balls. Denny and I watched anticipating the sweet taste of the popcorn balls when they were ready. How good they tasted!

The popped corn and the sweet odor of the syrup always filled our house with a delicious aroma that clung in the air. We could even smell it outside the house. Those popcorn balls were worth every minute of planting, raising, picking, shelling, fanning, popping, and cooking they took to make, not to mention the cleanup afterwards.

I still make popcorn balls from sorghum, and they taste exactly like they did when I was six and a half, going on seven:

SORGHUM POPCORN BALLS
1 C sugar
1 C water
1 C sorghum

Cook all three to "soft crack" stage. Then add:
2 T butter
1 tsp vanilla
1 tsp baking soda

Pour over the popped corn. Mix until fully coated. Let mixture cool slightly.

With buttered hands, shape into balls.

A Hard Lesson

It's six o'clock in the morning. Quickly I tiptoe into my parents' bedroom.

"Momma...Momma wake up!" I say.

Momma opens her eyes. "What is it, Joyce?"

"My tummy hurts...I'm gonna throw up!"

She took me the few steps to the bathroom and showed me how to lean over the toilet. Nothing happened.

"I'm awful cold, Momma."

She led me back to the bedroom and put me under the covers where she had slept. It was warm and comforting to me. My dad was still in bed and he asked Momma what the problem was.

"I'm not sure," she answered him.

Turning back to me she asked, "Joyce did you eat any of the Wealthy apples that I told you were green even though they looked red?"

"Just a little one with salt on it...not very much. Oh, my tummy hurts!" I started to cry.

"I guess each of the children will have to go through this before they learn," my dad said. "Do we have any Castor Oil?"

"Yes," said Momma, "but I will wait until she empties her stomach before I give it to her. Otherwise she won't keep it down. She's falling asleep. I'll go fix breakfast now."

I was safe and warm in Momma and Daddy's bed. It wasn't long before I woke up and cried, "I'm gonna throw up! Mommmaaaaaaa!"

Daddy jumped out of bed, grabbed me up, and had my head over the toilet just in the nick of time.

"Ruby! Ruby!" my dad called.

Momma came running into the bathroom. She waited until I settled down, then washed my face and led me back to her bed. This time I was given instructions to go to the bathroom by myself and not to wait for someone to be with me. I fell asleep.

Sometime later I woke up and could hear George and John talking with Denny who was playing in the sandbox. (Our sandbox had wooden sides and was not far from the west window of Momma and Daddy's bedroom.)

I heard Denny say, "Tell Joyce to come play. I made a big hill for the car."

John said, "Joyce ate green apples yesterday and now she's sick. She can't come play with you today."

"But I want her to. I'll let her play with my blue car."

I didn't hear the rest of their conversation because Momma came bearing the sure cure for green apple belly-ache—Castor Oil. She told me to open my mouth and to swallow immediately what she was about to put in it. I obediently opened my mouth and she quickly poured in the most vile-tasting liquid.

"Close your mouth! Swallow! Quickly! Swallow right now!" she said.

74

I started to heave and Momma said, "Don't do that, take a breath, here, take a bite of this. Chew it up quickly!"

It was a strawberry covered in a sweet syrup. Whatever it was did change the awful taste in my mouth. I shivered as I laid back in the bed exhausted.

The Castor Oil didn't take long to work its way through my system. Very soon I found myself sitting on the toilet for the results while leaning over the edge of the bathtub for the original problem! Needless to say, I spent most of that day traveling from Momma and Daddy's bedroom to the bathroom.

Today whenever I bite into an apple and it tastes "tart," as far as I'm concerned, it's a green apple and I spit it out. I always tell myself, *I learned this lesson once—the hard way!*

The Leaf House

By mid-October, the newness of school had worn off and life had settled into its usual routine. The splendors of fall, however, were just beginning. The red and yellow maple and elm leaves were falling and accumulating everywhere. How I loved to rake up a pile of leaves and "fall" into them!

One time Denny and I raked up a pile of leaves and made them into a floor plan of a house. I placed my little rocker in what was the living room and sat there rocking my doll. Soon my friend LaVonne McDivitt joined us and she and I played house, taking turns rocking the baby. We also made grown-up conversation:

"Hello. So nice of you to come visit. Please come in. How are you?"

"I'm just fine except for a little lumbago in my back."

"Oh, you poor thing! I hope it's not catching."

"How's the baby?"

"The baby's been sick. All she does is cry and I have to hold her all the time. I think she is teething because she slobbers and chews on everything, including me!"

On and on went our pretend conversation. It wasn't long until Denny had had enough and went off to play with the neighbor kids.

Soon afterwards LaVonne left and Gail Goodwin came over. She didn't enter my leaf house through the door, but stepped over the leaf wall! I didn't understand why she couldn't see the door.

Gail sat on the ground. She asked me, "Where is the little cupboard I gave you?"

I answered, "It's in my room upstairs. Momma told me to bring in all my furniture from the playhouse because Halloween is so near. I have to take this chair back into the house when I'm done playing."

"Are you going out on Halloween?"

"Oh no. Momma and Daddy said we have to stay home. They said we could have popcorn and make fudge." *Which is more fun anyway,* I thought.

Gail said, "Last year someone upset Mrs. Palmer's outhouse."

"Yeah, I heard about it. She came over and asked George and John to upright it. They sure looked funny at one another when she asked for help. Dorothy was with them when they upset it, so John asked her to help upright it, but she didn't want to help. Said she might fall into the pit!" (Dorothy was Gail's sister.) I laughed. "I wonder why she said that, but that's all I heard. John and George did go over and set up Mrs. Palmer's outhouse."

Gail stayed in my leaf house until suppertime, then left for home. I picked up my doll from under her "leaf" bed, put her in my little rocker, and drug both through the front door of my leaf house and onto the front porch.

I took one last look at my leaf house. The wind had picked up and had already blown one of the outside walls away. I waved goodbye to my leaf house and went indoors.

Brothers Are Forever

One night I was lying in bed about half asleep when I heard the hall floor squeak. This usually meant someone was there. I opened my eyes, but saw nothing. A moment later, I heard a rustling noise. I opened my eyes again and three white ghosts were silently dancing and moving about my room! I let loose with a blood-curdling scream and the three ghosts bolted out the door.

Daddy and Momma heard running overhead so they came upstairs to investigate. George and John were both in their room asleep. They peeked into Denny's room, but he was sound asleep, too. But something wasn't right. So Daddy turned on the lights and got the boys out of bed. I could hear him questioning them.

"George, did you hear Joyce scream?"

George replied, "No Daddy."

"John, did you hear Joyce scream?"

John replied, "No Daddy."

"Dennis, did you hear Joyce scream?"

Denny replied, "No Daddy."

Of course they never heard me scream. But, Momma searched their beds where she discovered three sheets wadded up into balls.

I didn't get up to see what exactly went on, but I could hear Daddy giving the boys a talking to. Denny was crying, probably afraid he was going to be spanked. I clearly heard promises not to ever, ever scare Joyce again. However, it wasn't long before George and John were back to tormenting their little sister.

A couple of weeks later, I was playing with my friend LaVonne McDivitt at her house. (An alley separated the McDivitt property from the Daniels' and I lived next door to Mrs. Daniels.) Normally, LaVonne would walk with me to the stump by the alley and then each of us would run as fast as we could for home. This day, however, we were so engrossed with play that I didn't notice it growing dark outside. I heard Momma call me at the same time Mrs. McDivitt called LaVonne. She couldn't walk with me to the stump! I was downright scared to walk home after dark! There were all kinds of spooky things—like trees—that could reach down and grab you. Then there were bears hiding around peeking at you. I thought, *Maybe if I run the bears won't get me.*

I got to the middle of the alley when suddenly a tree grabbed me! Then two bears threw a gunnysack over my head and proceeded to drag me down the alley! I was too scared to breathe or to holler as my kidnappers began to carry me. Just as quickly, they dropped me and took off. I scrambled out of the sack and ran for home.

Somehow I knew it couldn't have been trees and bears that caught me and stuffed me in that sack. I ran into the house. John and George were both laying on the floor in the living room listening to the radio. They pretended not to see me. I felt like kicking them both, but knew if I did, I'd be in big trouble.

So, before I went to bed, I snuck into their room, stole their slingshots, and hid them at the back of the hall closet. *That'll show them,* I thought. The next day, when George asked Momma if she'd seen his slingshot, I pretend to be busy playing with my dolls. I thought, *Maybe tomorrow I'll tell them where their slingshots are IF they tell me they are sorry for what they did to me!*

I don't remember the outcome of that incident, but do remember another like it. John and George both had made noisemakers out of large wooden spools from Momma's sewing basket. (These noisemakers were made by cutting notches in both ends of a spool, tying string carefully at one end, and then winding the string tightly around the spool. Then a long nail was inserted in the spool's hole. When held by the nail against a window, the string pulled quickly, which caused the noisemaker to send up an awful racket that would bring most people out of their chairs to investigate.)

One day close to Halloween, John said I could play with his noisemaker. I'd seen him and George use them many times, so that night I decided to try it on our living room window. The boys thought it was funny. But Daddy and Momma didn't think it was funny and neither did I when they were done with me! That was the first, last, and only time I used a spool noisemaker. After that, I firmly decided that someday when I get as big as George and John, I'll get them back good.

No doubt Momma and Daddy grew weary of the sibling squabbles that took place when we were children. Thankfully, such things are only a part of growing up.

The Coal Furnace

Every evening at suppertime, Momma would call us and we children were expected to wash our hands before appearing at the table. Denny and I often washed our hands under the bathtub faucet because George and John, being bigger than us, would push us aside, and hog the sink. Nevertheless, there was always warm water because Momma would light the gas water heater in the basement about an hour before Daddy came home. (When Daddy came home from work, he would normally take a bath, change his clothes, and then sit in his chair to read the newspaper, *The Perry Daily Chief*.) After supper, whoever was to have a bath that night did so and then Momma would shut off the heater.

This heater was connected to a coal furnace by pipes that ran through the side of its fire bowl. This meant that in the winter we never had to light the gas burner to heat our water. Sometimes when the water got very hot it would make a popping sound in the pipes.

Daddy would say, "Joyce, go run some hot water into the bathtub to relieve the pressure."

Sometimes I had to use a towel as a hot pad holder to shut off the water.

It was up to George or John to stoke the furnace regularly. ("Stoke" means to stir the fire inside a furnace, before adding the fuel.) They took turns shoveling the coal into the furnace to keep it burning. Once in awhile they would let me put in a shovel full. What a treat!

When the house began to cool down, Daddy would say, "John, go put two shovels of coal in the furnace and, on your way, take the coal bucket from the kitchen down with you."

This meant that John was expected to carry a bucket of coal upstairs when he came back.

Every evening Daddy would ask him, "Did you empty the ashes from the kitchen stove after supper?"

If he hadn't, John had to take them out in the dark. That would scare me if I had to go out in the dark by myself. Ghosts and goblins were out there just waiting to grab me. I know because I heard one moving around the chicken house making scratching noises one night. I was with John and he told me it was probably a ghost looking for me. I ran as fast as I could to get into the house, then I peeked out the back door to see if the ghost got John. But, all I heard was laughing!

Before going to bed, Daddy would "bank" the furnace for the night. He started by shaking the grates to let the ashes fall down away from the fire into an enclosed area. From here the ashes could be removed easily by opening a small door. He shoveled the ashes into wooden bushel baskets then sprayed water over them to make sure there were no hot coals remaining. Then he selected a few large pieces of coal to place on top of the remaining hot coals. Next he closed the damper, which would allow the fire to burn slowly for a long time. In this way the furnace stayed warm all night. When morning came, Daddy repeated this process. Soon warm air was coming out of all the registers. How nice and cozy it was! Because we were little and still needed help dressing, Denny and I were allowed to bring our clothes downstairs and dress by the kitchen stove. Momma was usually busy cooking breakfast, but still managed to help us.

On Wednesdays and Saturdays, Daddy and the boys carried the baskets of ashes from the basement to a place near the garage where the ground dropped off about two feet. (My dad was trying to fill in this space.)

When a supply of coal was ordered, Momma always reminded Mr. Tack at Denniston & Partridge Lumber Company to tell the haulers to spray water on it in order to keep the dust to a minimum. There was a large iron door located on the foundation of our house below the kitchen that opened into our coal room in the basement. When the coal truck arrived, a chute was placed into the opening, and then men shoveled the coal from the truck into this room.

One time Daddy ordered the coal, but forgot to remind them to spray it. The men came and delivered the coal, and soon the whole house filled with dust! Momma was so upset she cried. We all pitched in—including my dad—to clean up the mess. My job was to wipe the bottom window sills and the top of the baseboards. John cleaned the top of the windows. He also helped Denny wipe down the furniture. Daddy carefully swept the floors and Momma followed him, using a wet mop. We didn't own a vacuum sweeper, so the living room rug was carried out to the clothes line and a wire rug beater was used to clean it.

(A "rug beater" was a wire contraption that was woven and rounded on the top end. It was flat but the wire ends were bent up and encased in a wooden handle to keep your hand from rubbing the rug. Whenever we hit the rug with the rug beater, the dust flew! George was especially good at using the rug beater—so much so that I remember Momma and Daddy cautioning him not to hit the rugs too hard because the fibers could break and then the rugs would be ruined.) When the job was done, the house and basement were clean. Daddy never again forgot to remind Mr. Tack to have the coal sprayed with water before a delivery!

The Dinner Plate

One November morning, I woke up earlier than usual. The delicious smell of baked turkey and dressing filled my nose. Turning over, I looked out the window and saw the ground covered with fresh snow. I thought, *It's Thanksgiving! It's Thanksgiving! And we're going to have turkey today! And Momma has promised the wishbone to Denny and me!!*

Softly I hummed, "Over the river and through the woods, to Grandmother's house we go..." I thought for a moment. *I don't have a Grandmother's house to go to. They're both dead! But, Grandma Phillips is still living, and Daddy said she and Aunt Orpha would be here for dinner today.* (Grandma Phillips was actually my great-grandmother. Daddy was her grandson. Orpha was my dad's sister.)

Jumping out of bed, I grabbed my clothes and ran down the hall to the stairs. I could hardly contain myself and make my feet touch each step. I stopped abruptly at the bottom. The house was quiet. Where was everyone?

The dining room table was already set. Hurriedly, I walked through the living room, then into Momma and Daddy's bedroom; no one was there. Deciding to get dressed, I raced into the bathroom and closed both doors.

89

I quickly used the toilet, then washed my hands and face, and put on my clothes.

I hustled out to the kitchen and there was Momma working quietly. I slid into Daddy's chair at the end of the table where a bowl of oatmeal and a glass of milk were waiting for me.

"Where are Daddy and the boys?" I asked.

She answered, "They are taking some candy to Roy Heel."

"I wanted to go too, Momma. I ain't seen Mr. Heel in a long time."

She turned. "Joyce, you must not use that word 'ain't.' You must say, 'I haven't seen.' Also, you can't go every time your dad takes the boys."

I mulled this over and decided the boys got to go lots more than I did. I thought, *Why do I have to have so many brothers? They always get everything, and they try to make me mind them, too!*

I continued eating and watched Momma as she worked with the bread dough in front of her. She pinched off some dough from the mound in the bowl and carefully rolled it into a ball. After she'd made several little balls, Momma gently placed them three at a time into one of the wells in a cupcake pan. She called these "clover leaf rolls," and they did make me think of clover leaves, each with their three parts. Once the pans were full, she put them into the warming oven above the stove.

As I finished my milk, I heard Daddy's little pickup rumbling around the side of the house. A few minutes later the kitchen door flew open and a cold gust of wind swept through as the boys noisily made their entrance. When

Daddy came in Momma said he was to pick up Grandma Phillips at eleven o'clock. I looked at the clock on the wall, but didn't know how to tell time very well. When the hands were between two numbers, I could never figure out which two they are closest to!

Daddy took off his coat and went to the living room. I followed him.

"Daddy?"

"Yes, Joyce?"

"Can I go with you to pick up Grandma Phillips?"

He sat down in his chair. "No, Joyce, I'm taking George. But, you can watch for us to return and hold doors open for us. Would you like to do that?"

"Yes Daddy," I said, hiding my disappointment.

He and George left a short while later. It felt like they'd never get back. Finally they returned with Grandma Phillips. Once she saw me, she smiled and said,

"I've brought you something, Joyce. It's something your daddy's mother, your Grandma Anderson, gave me as a present many years ago. I would like for you to have it."

Momma handed me Grandma's coat to lay on her and Daddy's bed. I scampered away with it and hurried back to see what Grandma had for me.

When I returned, she was seated in a chair. She handed me a package wrapped in brown butcher paper and tied with white string.

I took the package and opened it. Inside was the most beautiful dinner plate I'd ever seen.

"Oh, how pretty. Thank you Grandma. I like it!"

I turned to Momma. "Momma! Momma! Come see the plate Grandma gave to me."

91

I held up the plate. "Look at all the pink and yellow roses it has on it. Can I eat off it today? Can I Momma, can I, huh?"

Momma admired the plate, took it to the kitchen to wash it, and placed it on the table where I was to sit.

Meanwhile, Aunt Orpha arrived. Momma greeted her courteously even though they often did not get along. As she took off her coat, Aunt Orpha greeted Grandma Phillips and Daddy as well as the boys. I caught her eye and smiled but she looked the other way. Momma handed me her coat and I took it into the bedroom and laid it carefully on the bed. When I returned to the dining room, Aunt Orpha was standing over the table fingering my dinner plate.

"What a beautiful plate, Ruby. The pattern looks familiar. Where did it come from?" she asked Momma.

"It was a present from Grandma to Joyce," Momma replied.

Momma returned to the kitchen leaving me alone with Aunt Orpha. She eyed me coldly before turning to talk with Grandma.

When it was time to eat, Daddy made the boys wait to be seated until he seated Grandma next to him. I was to sit next to her, but before I could get there Aunt Orpha slid onto the chair in front of my new rose covered plate.

"No, no that's my place to eat!" I cried.

She scowled at me. "Sit down and be quiet. I'm going to stay put."

I let loose with a wail in protest.

Grandma said, "Orpha, Joyce asked to sit next to me today and eat from her new plate."

Aunt Orpha unfolded my napkin and laid it on her lap. Ignoring Grandma's comment she said, "If she were my daughter she'd be excused from the table for pouting and being rude to a guest."

At this, I went down on my knees sobbing and crawled to the corner by Momma's sewing machine where I covered my head with my arms and continued my wailing. For the next several minutes I could hear my Grandma, my aunt, and my dad talking loudly with one another. Finally Daddy said, "Enough! Orpha, you will move and let Joyce take her seat."

For a moment there wasn't a sound other than the ticking of the kitchen clock. *When Daddy talks like that he means business,* I thought.

I peered out from under my arm to see that my chair was vacant. Daddy said, "It's all right, Joyce. Please come to the table so we can have our Thanksgiving meal."

Slowly I got up and took my place. I didn't dare look at Aunt Orpha, who was now seated uncomfortably between George and John and whose gaze felt even colder than before. Once everyone was eating, Grandma slipped her hand under the table and gave my knee a reassuring squeeze.

I don't remember what we had for dessert or who won when Denny and I broke the wishbone, but after dinner we children were given ten cents each and allowed to walk downtown to the show. What a treat! We had so much fun we stayed to see the show twice! When we returned, Grandma and Aunt Orpha had left and my beautiful plate was washed and dried and locked safely away in Momma's china cabinet. Years later I learned Aunt Orpha believed the dinner plate to be rightfully hers since it was a gift from her mother, but apparently my Grandma Phillips believed that a gift was a gift.

Winter

Christmas, 1927

Christmas of 1927 is the first I can remember. George was seven, John was five, I was three and a half, and Denny was one. One morning about a week or so before Christmas, I woke up very early. I thought it was Christmas day, but did not hear anyone up. Quietly, I slipped out of bed and walked down the hall to the stairs. I made the few steps down to the landing and looked into the living room. It was so dark I could barely see the outline of the Christmas tree. No, it wasn't Christmas morning. Disappointed, I returned to my room and my warm bed.

This happened several mornings in a row before one evening my dad told me,

"Tomorrow morning will be Christmas, Joyce, and Santa will bring you something nice. Don't you think Santa would like some milk? Why don't you get some ready for him?"

I got a glass from the pantry, brought the milk in from the back porch, and prepared to pour Santa a glass. My dad came into the kitchen to see how I was getting along.

"Joyce, I don't think Santa will have time to drink a whole glass. It would be better if you put a little in a saucer and then left it on the top basement step for him. He will probably come in the outside cellar door anyway."

At that time it didn't occur to me that we had apples, potatoes, squash, pumpkins, and onions stored on the cellar steps, or that Santa was supposed to come down the chimney. So I poured a little milk onto the saucer and Daddy helped me get it to the cellar door and place it on the top step next to the wall.

The next morning I could hear my two older brothers talking so I slipped out of bed, tiptoed down the hall, and quietly descended the steps to the landing. There I stood watching what was going on in the living room. The lights on the Christmas tree were on. I stood there transfixed by the myriad of colors reflected by the lights on the walls and ceiling of the living room. The whole room was bathed in a very colorful soft glow.

Momma said, "Joyce, come on downstairs and see what Santa left for you behind the tree!"

I went into the living room, but couldn't comprehend what all was going on. Tissue paper was strewn all over the floor, and each of my brothers had a toy in their hands. Denny was holding a stuffed monkey and was making its head go up and down and side to side by turning its tail.

George said, "Over here, Joyce. Look!"

I didn't see anything but the tree with all its lights. John got up from the floor, walked over to me, and took hold of my hand to lead me around the huge tree.

"Come Joyce, see what Santa left for you!" He reached out and pulled something from behind the tree. "Look, Joyce, look!"

Then I saw it. A doll buggy with a little doll and blanket in it! I instantly became very interested in that doll and buggy. Eagerly I joined my brothers on the floor to examine all these new toys that were not there last night when I went to bed.

(The Santa Claus myth is a delightful story told to children by parents for various reasons. One being an effective leverage for extracting good behavior from overly excited children, another is the pleasure derived from playing the game of make-believe. Even older children sometimes go along and don't blow the whistle on Santa until a younger sibling starts expressing disbelief by questioning Santa's ability to perform all the wonderful feats attributed to him.

In 1927, we had a red kitty who lived in the furnace room of the basement. I didn't realize until several years later that she was the recipient of the saucer of milk put there for "Santa." Unfortunately, the following spring that kitty went missing. My dad told me she took a pound of butter and left home. Once again, I believed him! I do remember feeling badly, though, as the kitty didn't even tell me goodbye.)

Holiday Decorating

Daddy had many sample books from which he sold wallpaper. He always gave me the discontinued books to play with. I would cut collars and cuffs from the prettier pages and keep them to wear with my "dress-up" clothes. I also cut doilies out of some pages for my tea tray, but could never play outdoors with them because of the wind. I usually played with the books in the turn of the staircase. This was an activity I enjoyed when there was no one around to play with me, and I never was lonely in this world of make-believe.

I had paper dolls—cut from Momma's *Delineator* or *McCall's* magazines—mounted on pieces of cardboard to make them stand up. I would dress these dolls in their finest and line them up on the stairs. They were often my guests—or fellow guests—at a party or reception for elegant people. Wearing my long "dress-up" dress with its paper collar and cuffs, I would have tea with famous women in far away places. One time I was a special guest of the queen, and sat beside her at her coronation in England! Mostly I would clunk up and down the stairs in Momma's old high heels. I would carry my cardboard spectacles mounted on a long handle in my right hand and a fan made from wallpaper in my left hand. I would peer through the spectacles as I acknowledged the dignitaries lined up to watch my entrance down the steps! My return to reality was usually a call from my mother urging me to pick up my playthings before Daddy came home.

One holiday season, Denny and I chose brightly colored pages from the books to cut into strips and make paper chains. This kept us busy for many hours, and we never seemed to tire of it. What a racket we made going up and down the stepladder and dragging it across the hardwood floor from window to window, then crawling from a chair onto the dining room table to reach the chandelier, which hung in the center of the room. Before we were finished, the large dining room was fully draped with chains. For some reason our older brothers did not appreciate the artistic talents of their younger brother and sister, so we were not allowed to decorate the living room. I thought, *How typical of older brothers! They think they know everything and usually get their own way. They're just jealous because we won't let them help us.*

Our conversations consisted mostly of instructions to each other on how to hang the chains and how much swag to put in them. Sometimes we tore the chains and would have to stop for repairs. We kept working until we'd covered every window and door. We used all the nails Momma had placed in each window and door to hang her winter clothesline. When the nails were all gone, we resorted to thumbtacks. When we finished, Denny and I laid on the paper-strewn floor, looked up at our beautiful artwork, and savored the moment.

(Of course we never realized what an awful mess we'd created for our mother to clean up. She was indeed a tolerant mother to allow two children to decorate her dining room in such a fashion. I don't ever remember Momma asking us to take the decorations down; just one day they would disappear. I never thought to ask why.)

Christmas, 1931

When we were small, my brothers and I very much believed in Santa, and with great anticipation looked forward to Christmas morning when we would receive the gifts he would place under the tree for us. And we looked forward to all the holiday food. We always celebrated with fresh fruit, Christmas candy, and a large assortment of nuts—English walnuts, Brazil nuts, pecans, and almonds. This was quite a treat as we only had canned fruit in the winter after the cold storage apples from the basement were gone, or black walnuts which, although plentiful, were often very difficult to crack.

One Christmas morning, to our surprise, we found by the tree a bushel basket of oranges, Red Delicious apples, bananas, and grapes. Sitting beside it was another basket full of assorted Christmas candy. It was more candy than I had ever seen! (I later learned that Bert McLaughlin had cleaned out his grocery store on Christmas Eve, and Daddy had brought home the excess for us to enjoy.)

This particular Christmas I was seven years old, and my gift from Santa was twin baby dolls in a small wicker basket. There was a lace-trimmed pillow under their heads and a small lacy coverlet over them. Their heads, hands,

105

and feet were made of porcelain, while the bodies were made of muslin. They wore white lace-trimmed dresses and lacy bonnets with pink ribbon bows neatly tied under their chins. Tiny white stockings adorned their feet and legs, and each wore a diaper of soft flannel. How beautiful they looked nestled in their little basket! I knew what a treasure I had and wondered what my friends would say when they saw them. I was more than pleased with my dolls. Why, I was certain no little girl in all of Perry had received such a wonderful gift! I hugged them to me, basket and all, as I pictured in my mind where they would sleep in my playhouse come summer. I softly hummed to them as I rocked them in their basket. How happy I was! Santa had truly chosen the right gift for me.

My younger brother Denny had been given a rather heavy metal airplane that he had wanted for some time. It was black and had orange markings on it. It was a real beauty and very special to him. He handled it most carefully as he played with it on the floor. He pushed the airplane to me, and as I turned it around to push it back to him, a wheel fell off. I put my basket of dolls on the floor, and picked up the plane to reattach the wheel. Hard as I tried, I could not get it to stay on. I asked our oldest brother, George, to fix it. He kept trying, but the wheel repeatedly fell off the axle. At this point Denny was very upset. He proceeded to grab one of my dolls, pull off her head, and throw the body down in front of me. I sat there stunned, unable to believe what I was seeing.

Just then George said, "Here it is Denny, all fixed!"

I kept looking at my doll laying in two parts with her sawdust stuffing spilling onto the carpet. I kept thinking,

Denny, how could you do such an awful thing?! Unfortunately, he was too young at the time to realize how much pain his "get even" action had caused me. Momma and Daddy had told me before never to hit him because he was my little brother. This, of course, did nothing to relieve the ache I was feeling inside. I could not sort out my feelings. I did not hate Denny for what he had done, yet this overwhelming feeling of great loss kept tearing at me over something that shouldn't have happened.

Quietly I picked up my dolls, and carried them to Momma. She did her best to repair the broken doll, but the head always remained loose; she was never the same. Even though it was Christmas—supposedly a time of great joy—I felt grief, not unlike the initial grief that grips one following the death a loved one. Yet, because I was a child, I couldn't figure out at the time why I was so sad.

The Valentine Box

One morning in 1932, I noticed that Miss Ortwig, our third grade teacher, had the most "beautifulest" box sitting on her desk. It was red and was covered in red hearts on lace paper. It even had little red ribbon bows on each side and a large slit in the top. Since it was early in the month of February, we all knew what it was—the Valentine Box!

Miss Ortwig shooed us away from the box and told us to take our hats, coats, mittens, scarves, and overshoes to the cloak room. Then we were to go to our seats, sit down, fold our hands on the desk, and be quiet. School was "taking up" for the day. Roll call was taken and then we recited the Pledge of Allegiance.

After we sat down, Miss Ortwig talked to us about the box. She told us we would be making valentines to put into the box. Then the box would be opened on the last day of school before Valentine's Day, and the valentines would be passed out.

The next afternoon Miss Cunningham came for her weekly art class with us. She brought with her pieces of red and white paper with hearts drawn on them. She carefully cut out one of the hearts to show us how to stay within the

109

lines. Then we were each given a pair of blunt-nosed scissors, and started cutting out our hearts.

I looked across the isle and saw Jack Audas intent on his work while biting his lower lip.

Miss Cunningham went to the blackboard and wrote the words, "To My Valentine," and also, "From Your Friend." I chose my white crayon to write these inscriptions on my card and then added my name. She also explained to us that most people gave valentines to their friends to show friendship. She told us to put the name of someone in the class on the back and we could place our valentines in the box. I kept my hand over the name on the one I made so I wouldn't be teased. I wrote the name of a classmate I knew wouldn't get very many.

With the scraps, Miss Cunningham showed us how to fold the paper and cut hearts freehand. We sure had some funny-looking hearts—short, skinny, lop-sided, and fat—but we had so much fun cutting them! The hour with Miss Cunningham was all too short.

As soon as she left, Miss Ortwig told us we could come up by rows to deposit our cards in the Valentine Box. She said it would be opened that Friday because Valentine's Day was on Sunday.

After school I hurried home to tell Momma what we had made and asked her if I was going to buy valentines for the rest of the kids in class. Momma suggested that this year I make valentines for my friends. I should have known she would say that. The winter of 1932 was not a time of plenty. We were in the grip of the Great Depression and most families did well just to have enough to eat. Store-bought valentines were a luxury few could afford.

110

The next day I brought home a small piece of red construction paper to work on. Momma looked at it and advised me not to cut out a small heart but to fold the paper to open like a book. She had a candy box that had lace edges on it. She carefully removed the lace and pasted it to the front side of my valentine. She carefully "mitered" the corners to make the lace look all one piece. It was so pretty! I intended to give it to Miss Ortwig. When Denny saw my valentine, he immediately wanted one for his teacher. Thoughtfully, Momma had saved enough materials for Denny to make one the next day.

On Friday morning we placed the last of our valentines inside the beautiful box. That afternoon, not long before school was dismissed for the weekend, Miss Ortwig asked Junior South and Jack Audas to deliver the valentines. Miss Ortwig lifted the top off the box, picked them up one by one, and announced the name of the recipient. The two boys delivered them to our desks. Of course, the popular kids received more than the rest of us. I looked over to see if the boy I had made the first one for had any others on his desk. As I had already guessed, there weren't very many. Inside I was glad I had made one for him.

Miss Ortwig received valentines from every one of us. She took the time to read them and to thank us individually. When we were dismissed, she thoughtfully gave the beautiful box to the one person who had received the fewest valentines. He had the biggest smile on his face; it really made him happy. I held my valentines in my hand as I walked home. I felt happy about the valentine exchange and was anxious to share it with Momma.

Christmas, 1932

This Christmas season I am eight years old. The Depression is heavy upon us. This was a very trying time for my parents. Our family had grown to five children and the birth of our youngest brother, David, had been difficult.

Momma had been in the hospital all summer long, so there hadn't been much processing of the garden produce. My older brothers had helped my dad dig the potatoes and store them on the steps of the basement's outdoor entry where they had also stored the apples wrapped in paper. The pumpkins had been carried in from the garden and stored on the basement floor. During the summer, Daddy and Mrs. Wykoff, our hired girl, had made strawberry sunshine jam. (This jam is made through a process of mixing sugar with the berries, placing them in a glass-covered container, and leaving them in the sun for a length of days.) How good it tasted on toast and clover leaf rolls.

In the fall, Daddy and the boys had gathered walnuts from the timber and hulled them using a hammer and a board. Usually Momma would crack a large pan of nuts and bring them to the kitchen table where we children would pick out the nut meats. She always checked our work to make sure there were no little shells in it. Then

Momma would make walnut cake, fudge, or divinity for us. But these goodies would not be plentiful during this holiday season. The surgery my mother underwent had left her weak. She was in need of household help, but had let her hired girl go. With the winter upon us, there was no painting and papering work for my father.

Thanksgiving being over, the turkeys, pumpkins, and pilgrims had been removed from the downtown shop windows. The worn and faded Christmas decorations from last year were brought out and placed in the windows for sale along with the new stock. At the intersection of Second and Warford Streets heavy red ropes crisscrossed the street from J. C. Penney's to the bank and from Spurgeon's department store to Ray B. Smith's drugstore. From the middle of these ropes hung a huge red bell. It had to be the biggest red bell ever made, or at least, the biggest I'd ever seen. The bell swung back and forth in the wind and I used to imagine it was ringing just for me. Christmas music— which at that time was comprised mostly of hymns—played repeatedly all day long through a loudspeaker fastened to one of the buildings. People on the street greeted one another with, "Merry Christmas!" And the clerks and shopkeepers would question we children about our behavior of late because, as we all knew, Santa didn't give gifts to disobedient children.

That year the Elks Club gave away bags of Christmas candy to all children who came to see Santa. My brothers and I joined the long line of children who climbed the front steps to the club, walked through the entry room containing the pool tables, and into the bar room where Santa was handing out the candy. Then we filed down the back steps to the outdoors. Daddy insisted we make only one trip through the line, and that we wear our heavy coats, scarves, hats, mittens, and overshoes. He knew that any child who came through the line without any one of these articles of clothing, would immediately be taken by an Elk member and questioned about his or her lack of appropriate attire. If any children proved to be in need, then they were taken downtown where the missing clothing would be purchased for them. (The Great Depression affected everyone, but some families were really in difficult straits. What a magnificent gesture for the men of the Elks Club no. 407 to care so deeply for the children in need at Christmas.)

This year Miss Cunningham put us to work making Christmas decorations. My classmates and I cut out trees, wreaths, candles, and bells from construction paper. These were used to decorate our classroom and the Christmas tree that stood in the corner of the room. Friday, December 23rd was the last day of school before the two-week Christmas vacation, and on that day we were allowed to take our decorations home with us. The tree was given to anyone who wanted it. The last fifteen minutes or so of class were spent singing Christmas carols, without the benefit of recorded music. I, along with several of my classmates, was moved by our singing. However, the feeling lasted only until we were dismissed and could hit the school grounds. We all dashed home with our construction paper decorations in hand.

Denny and I pinned our decorations to the dining room curtains because our older brothers didn't want to see our "handmade stuff" on the tree. Denny and I could not understand our brothers' lack of appreciation for our artwork. Momma told us to pin them to the dining room curtains where she could see them better. She thought what we made was the best she'd ever seen, even if our brothers did not!

In the middle bay window of our living room hung a red wreath with an electric candle in the center. This decoration was always hung and plugged in beginning December 1st. Our dad would not allow us to have a tree until closer to Christmas Eve. (I think he was afraid of fire. Our neighbors, the Hawks, had real candles on their tree, although I never saw them lit.) This year we had new strings of electric lights for our tree. Before Daddy brought the tree into the house, he sawed off the end, placed it in a bucket of wet sand, and then put the bucket inside a wooden cranberry box. The tree never fell over after being secured in this manner.

The next day was Christmas Eve and I was excited. Santa was coming to town at 2:00 PM and would throw candy to the children. My brothers and I were allowed to walk the twelve blocks to the library where Santa was to pass by. Because the weather was mild, the sidewalks were teeming with people. I remember standing on the sidewalk in front of the First National Bank with my brothers, when we heard the fire truck siren announcing Santa's arrival. The fire truck slowed down then stopped in the intersection and Santa started throwing candy.

Suddenly, the crowd surged behind me, pushing me into the street. The crowd from the other side met us in the middle and I found myself surrounded by people pushing at me from all sides. I didn't know where my brothers were and couldn't see anything as my face was pressed against a man's back pocket. Because I was wedged in so tightly, I couldn't raise my arms. Instantly I was afraid and started crying. I opened my mouth to scream when something caused me to look up. I could see a little patch of blue sky between the arms reaching over my head. The crowd behind me moved a little and I was able to reach my arm up and grab the man's pocket so I wouldn't fall down. The fear lessened as the people started moving away. To my dismay, Santa had already moved down the street and the people were following him.

I couldn't find my brothers so I walked home alone, sobbing most of the way. I remember thinking to myself, *Isn't Santa supposed to be for little kids like me?* I didn't get any candy that day. What I did receive is a frightening memory that resurfaces anytime I'm caught in a large pressing crowd.

January Thaw

January was always a cold month, but sometimes we would have a "thaw" that would melt the snow causing the water to puddle on the sidewalks and streets. At the corner of Fifth and North Streets, the water would flow quite deep. So the city would place an iron grate on the curb. This grate extended several feet into the street, making it possible to cross the water without getting our feet wet. My brothers and I always had our overshoes on, but sometimes the water was deep enough to go over their tops. This caused a problem for anyone who had a hole in his overshoes. Holes were not uncommon, as we wore our overshoes every day from the first cold spell or snow (whichever came first) until spring. They put up with as much wear and tear as our shoes did.

One Sunday afternoon, Momma and Daddy took Denny and me with them out to Herman and Dora Meier's house. George and John had something else to do so did not go with us. It had been cold for awhile, but because of a thaw, the day was quite warm.

Dorothy was happy to see us. We hadn't been there long before she said, "The 'crick' is still frozen over. Let's go play on it."

I said, "We have to ask Momma and Daddy."

Mr. Meier heard us talking and said, "It's safe for them. The ice is still firm."

(Hank Aleck, the man who lived in the cabin across the creek on the Meiers' land, often rode to town with Mr. Meier, so the creek condition was always watched closely.) We ran out the back door without our overshoes and were immediately caught and made to put them on. With four sets of eyes watching us, we couldn't get by with much!

Beaver Creek was a short distance from their house, just down the hill a ways. Anxious to play on the ice, we ran most of the way. Denny had on new overshoes that wouldn't slide, but Dorothy and I had no trouble as ours were worn. We ran fast and could slide quite a distance. Denny kept watching us as he struggled to slide only a foot or so. The next thing I knew, he slid past us laughing and waving his arms in the air. It wasn't difficult to understand how this could be—no overshoes!

Sometimes we ran fast, squatted down, wrapped our arms around our legs, then let go and slid on our backsides. Dorothy and I held one another's arms and spun around and around, faster and faster until we lost our balance and both of us went flying on our bottoms, sides, or stomachs, however we landed. Then Denny would join hands with us and we would run in a circle to see who could remain upright the longest. Sometimes we all went down in a pile, squealing, laughing, and hollering at one another.

We played on the ice until we heard our names being called. Of course we ignored the calls, but not for long. If Daddy started down the hill Denny and I would be in trouble. On the third call we waved our arms at him and started our last slide home. Denny had to remember to pick up and put on his overshoes before we left the creek. He tried and tried to get them on, but his shoes were so wet they kept sticking inside his overshoes. He finally got his feet inside far enough to walk and slowly the heels slipped into place.

We trudged back up the hill to Dorothy's house. Somehow it seemed much farther away than when we ran down to the creek earlier. We were no longer laughing or trying to see who could reach the house first. Three cold, wet, bedraggled children, worn to a frazzle, finally reached the back door and the haven of a warm house. The aroma of coffee met us and we knew Mrs. Meier had prepared a lunch for us to eat. She'd made sandwiches, cake, and milk for us kids, and coffee for the grown-ups. How good it tasted! We were really hungry after playing on the ice.

As I was eating, I noticed my dad looking at Denny's wet shoes. He didn't say anything until we started for home. Denny was given quite a lecture on "minding what you're told." (Disobedience was not tolerated in our household, and any "sassing" always guaranteed a spanking.)

Denny quickly said, "I'm sorry! I won't do it again!"

I'm not sure how "sorry" Denny was, but evidently it was convincing enough to escape being punished. When we arrived home, Denny propped his shoes against the hot air register to dry along with our mittens. Hopefully they would be dry to wear to school the next day.

Supper was leftovers from dinner. We children really wolfed them down. George and John were there and, as always, were very hungry. Daddy often said John had a hollow leg and I giggled every time because I used to think he really did! Momma had to set me straight on that one. Denny fell asleep at the table and Momma had to wake him so he could go to bed. That night it turned very cold and it snowed quite a bit. The next morning Denny was happy his shoes were dry to wear to school.

Fun on a Snowy Winter Day

One winter morning I awoke to find a heavy snow had fallen. Knowing school would be canceled, I quickly dressed and ran downstairs to the kitchen.

"Momma! Momma! It snowed last night! And it's still snowing! Can we go out and play in it? Please, Momma, please?"

"Joyce," Momma answered, "you may go outdoors, but please remember the difference between the words *can* and *may!*"

"Yes, Momma. I won't forget."

Momma was always correcting my English. (You'd think I ain't never been to school or nothin'!)

I turned to Denny. "Let's get our coats on!"

We hurriedly put on our heavy winter coats and hats and our long pants. We wound scarves around our faces, pulled on our overshoes, and grabbed our leather mittens we'd placed in front of the register to dry from being worn the day before. We scrambled out the front door to see who could jump the farthest into the snowdrift that ran in front of our house. Even though I was taller than Denny, sometimes his jump would beat mine.

We rolled in the snow and chased each other into the huge drift. We laughed at each other's dramatic entrances into the snow. Since the snow was soft, we could do cartwheels, somersaults, and dives off this drift without hurting ourselves.

Denny yelled, "Watch this, Joyce! Here I go, wheee!"

He lit flat on his stomach and slid down the drift. When he stood up he was covered with snow from head to toe. I laughed and laughed at him. Then it was my turn. Not wishing to get snow on my face, I ran and jumped sideways and slid to the bottom. I conceded that Denny's stunt was far superior to mine.

Tired from all the jumping, I decided to catch snowflakes in my mouth. Denny mimicked me. We must have been something to see—heads back, mouths open, all covered with snow. Next we decided to go to the side yard to make snow angels. We would each make one and then decide whose was best. Soon tired of this activity, we trudged to the house. Momma was waiting on the front porch with her broom in hand to sweep the snow from our clothes and overshoes before we could enter the house.

She'd say, "Raise your arm, turn sideways, turn around and please stand still!"

Once in awhile, the broom would get too close to our faces when she was brushing the snow from our heads. This always got our attention so we stood still and followed instructions. We hung up our wet clothes to dry and placed our mittens in front of the heat register. Then we raced each other to the living room to see who could get the best spot in front of the register there to get warm. Immediately a pushing and shoving match took place. Since

I wore a dress, it would billow out so Denny thought I was hogging the heat.

"Get over, Joyce. Let me have some heat!"

"I am over. Quit pushing me!"

"Momma!" we both howled.

Momma came into the room to "settle" us. She said, "You're both in front of the register, so why are you arguing over space?"

Suddenly another rush of heat caused my skirt to billow out. Denny hollered, "See, Momma, see her, she's hogging all the heat!"

"Joyce, hold your dress down on Denny's side," Momma said.

As I did so, the other side and the front flew up into my face. Momma said, "Joyce pull your skirt up a little on Denny's side and you both stand closer together."

It worked. When my skirt billowed out, it sort of funneled the heat towards Denny. Another argument was over, settled by Momma's reasoning.

After warming up, we placed checkers on the living room floor. Just then John came in and suggested we make "snow ice cream." Denny and I jumped to our feet, grabbed our coats, and ran out the back door with a pan to gather some clean snow. Momma carefully divided the snow into four glasses and poured cold milk mixed with sugar and vanilla over it. Actually, the end result looked more like slush than ice cream. Nevertheless, we enjoyed our snow treats.

John always teased Denny and me by saying we got into the "yellow" snow. Of course, this remark would make us mad. We'd holler, "We did not! We're gonna tell Momma on you if you say it again!" But John was careful not to tease us too much. Being older and wiser, he always knew when to quit before he got into trouble.

John's Cookout

One warm afternoon in early December, I sat in the yard and waited for John to come home from school. He looked excited as he ran into the house, so of course I followed him. He went into the kitchen, selected several potatoes, and started peeling them.

"What are you doing?" I asked.

"I'm hungry. I'm going to fry me some potatoes," he answered.

"Can I have some, too?"

"Yes, if you help me a little, like going to the porch and getting me kindling wood and some larger pieces."

"You want big logs like Momma puts in the stove?"

"No, just little stuff like what's in the box at the end of the stacked woodpile."

I gathered the kindling and wood pieces in the skirt of my dress and followed John outdoors to the side yard.

He found three bricks and arranged them on the ground—one on each side and one to the back leaving the front open—to make a little "stove." I handed him the kindling and he carefully piled it on the ground inside the bricks. Then he laid some of the larger pieces on the top and poured a little kerosene over them. He pulled a box of

127

matches from his pocket, lit one, and held it to the pile. When it started burning well he placed the rest of the larger pieces on top.

When he had the fire going "good," he placed Momma's long handled frying pan (called a "spider") over the fire. In it were the sliced potatoes, a little lard, salt, and pepper.

As they fried, the aroma was absolutely tantalizing. I could hardly wait for them to be done so I could eat some! With a small spatula, John turned the potatoes over and they were a beautiful shade of reddish brown. They looked ready to eat, but John said, "No, not yet."

After the potatoes cooked a little longer, he lifted the frying pan from the brick stove and announced they were ready.

He took a fork from his pocket, speared several slices, and handed it to me.

"Be careful, they're still hot," he cautioned.

I waited until the potatoes were cool enough to touch. Mmmmmm...they smelled so good! I put the potatoes into my mouth and started chewing. Aaauuugh! Gag!! The potatoes tasted like kerosene smells! Quickly I spit them out onto the ground.

John gave me an incredible look of disbelief and said, "What's the matter? Is something wrong? Don't you like my cooking?"

"It tastes awful! It's the worst thing I ever tasted! Worse than Castor Oil!"

John kept on eating his potatoes. As I hurried to the house to rid my mouth of that terrible taste, he called, "Joyce, you just don't appreciate fine outdoor cooking!!"

(I can still vividly see a ten-year-old John squatting by his brick stove cooking potatoes. Years later, Momma had the frying pan silver-plated and gave it to John as a birthday present.)

Christmas, 1933

It's 1933, and I'm nine years old. The Depression has become almost unbearable, and many people are hungry and cold. Some of our neighbors are accepting welfare. This was a difficult step for them to take, to swallow their pride and "go on the county." (Those in my parents' generation were hard workers; they took pride in all they did, and accepted full responsibility for the welfare of their families. To accept charity was a terrible blow to many people's sense of self-worth.) As a result, some men walked with their shoulders sloped and their heads hung down. But they had no choice; their families had nothing to eat.

Early Christmas morning we children scampered downstairs. Each of us found one gift under the Christmas tree. Momma always wrapped our gifts in white tissue paper and wrote our names on them. I opened my box to find a beautiful set of china dishes: four plates, four cups, four saucers, a teapot, a sugar and a creamer. They were an orange brown color with a sunset scene painted on them. I was quite thrilled as now I had a real set of dishes for my playhouse! I carefully unwrapped them and set them for a make-believe tea party on the floor. When Denny grew tired of playing tea party with me, I gathered my dishes and stacked them neatly on the bay window sill for safe-keeping.

I sat on the floor and looked at them. They were so pretty; how happy I was to have them. When my little friend LaVonne came to my tea parties next summer, we would have real dishes on the table! I would keep my dishes in the little gray cupboard and together we would set the table for our party. Maybe we'd have real cookies or crackers with water for our tea. Because it was winter, all my playhouse furniture was in my bedroom. Too bad I continued day-dreaming and didn't take the dishes up to my room!

For some reason, John decided he was going to adjust an ornament on the tree (or perhaps a light was out). He jumped up onto the window sill, fixed whatever needed fix-ing, then stepped backwards into my dishes and sent them shattering onto the hardwood floor! Only two cups, one saucer, and two plates remained unbroken. The rest were shattered, as were my dreams of a beautiful tea party with LaVonne. As he helped me pick up the pieces, John kept telling me over and over and over how sorry he was and that he didn't mean to step backwards into them. I didn't want John to feel so badly. My loss seemed great to me, but his remorse was obviously really hurting him.

Momma reassured me the dishes were "open stock" and I would get replacements. Although we were blessed to have an abundance of food, in 1933, there was no money for "extras." (I think Momma had bought those dishes one piece at a time over a whole year. She was never able to re-place them.)

Sliding Down Haunted Hill

"Momma, can I go play on Haunted Hill? Denny wants to go, too. Can we take the large scoop shovel from the basement? We'll be home by dark and won't be late for supper. Can we go, Momma? Please?" I asked.

Having received permission, I ran to get the large shovel. I didn't dare ask for the small one because it fit the coal furnace door and was used to shovel coal onto the fire. The larger one was used to remove ashes from the bottom door, but the little one could be used there as well. The only time we were allowed to use the small shovel was to remove snow from the sidewalk. We had to then return it immediately to the coal room.

"Haunted Hill" was on the northeast corner of Sixth and Dewey Streets. It was a very high hill that had an old, badly deteriorated house on the very top. The big kids told me they had looked in one of the windows of the house and saw a man lying on the floor with a knife stuck in his back. They said that robbers, murderers, and kidnappers of little girls were hiding in there. I believed them! I was so afraid of this old house I would not walk near it unless my big brothers were with me.

133

Denny and I went out the front door and tried—without success—to slide down the small incline in front of our house. Denny scrambled down to the sidewalk and promptly sat on the shovel waiting for me to pull him to the alley. Then he pulled me in the shovel for a short distance, and when we got to Haunted Hill, most of the neighborhood kids were already taking turns sliding down the hill towards Sixth Street. We could hear them shouting and laughing before we left home. I saw barricades in the street shutting off traffic. Several of the neighborhood boys had received permission from all the people affected by the barricades, so the city closed off the street for us to play. (There really wasn't much traffic back then. Few people had cars in the early thirties.)

We each took turns carrying the shovel up the steepest part of the hill. Denny went down the hill first, while I stood in line to take my turn. Some of the kids laughed as he slid sideways before he reached the bottom. He carried the shovel back up to me and took his place at the end of the line. I sat on the shovel holding the handle in front of me, my feet on the ground pushing, but I wasn't going anywhere. One of the big kids started pushing on my shoulders and away I went flying and bumping on the ice to the bottom of the hill. What a thrill! Hurriedly, I got out of the way for the next slider to come downhill.

When I went back uphill, some of the boys said, "Want a ride on our sled? We'll let you have one sled ride for two shovel rides."

"I think it should be even up," I said.

"Nope," they said. "One sled ride for two of your dumb shovel rides."

"If it's so dumb," I said, "then why do you want to ride it?"

"If you don't give us two for one," they said, "we won't let you ride our sled ever!"

Denny said, "C'mon Joyce, I wanna ride the sled!"

Reluctantly I agreed, so they gave Denny and me the sled for one ride down the hill. Denny took the sled, gave a short run, and flopped down on it. As he came down the slope to where I was standing, I jumped onto his back to share the ride. We went a half block before stopping! We returned the sled, and then each of the big boys took a turn on our shovel. When they brought it back, they offered to give Denny a circle ride. Denny sat in the shovel holding onto the handle. One of the boys gripped the hand piece with both hands and slowly started turning it in circles, picking up speed. He turned faster and faster until Denny spilled over, bumping his head and shoulder on the ice. He started to cry. One of the boys called him a big baby. Since our older brothers were not there to stick up for us, I thought I could whack that boy with the shovel and easily run for home. But, I knew if Momma and Daddy found out I was in a "street fight" with a boy, I would never be allowed to play on Haunted Hill again. This was a tough choice to make! Since it was growing dark and we were tired, cold, and hungry, I decided to let it go and told Denny it was time for us to go home.

We hurried past the haunted house, down the back hill, and into the alley. We were too exhausted to even pull one another in the shovel. As we stepped onto the porch, we could smell the tantalizing aroma of supper. It gave us a spurt of energy to broom the snow off our clothes and boots before we entered the house. We carefully placed our boots near the kitchen stove, hung our coats on the coat hanger, and put our mittens on the floor in front of the register to dry overnight. I leaned the shovel against the cellar door for the next person going to the basement to return to the coal room.

We washed our hands and faces before taking our seats at the supper table. Our father asked the same blessing we had heard for as far back as I could remember. We had all memorized it because we never knew if he would call upon us to give it. This night he chose to give it himself: "We give thanks to Thee, Heavenly Father, for this blessing. We ask it in Jesus' name. Amen."

Truly, for such young children, we were grateful; but because we were so hungry, we could hardly wait to begin eating. Since decorum reigned at our mother's table, we waited until the food was passed to us before we helped ourselves. Momma always served potatoes and gravy with vegetables and meat for our evening meal. There was always some kind of canned fruit for dessert—sometimes even a fruit pie—but the biggest treat of all was when she made black walnut bread. It was so good it surely must have been food for royalty. Momma always cut it so everyone would have the same size piece with none left over.

Denny and I sat on a narrow bench behind the table— and later our younger brother David, too—while George and John had chairs on the other side. Daddy sat at one end of the table and Momma sat at the other end next to the stove. My seat was next to an east window, which sometimes was very cold. Momma would take my father's sheep skin coat and put it on the bench for me to sit on. I was never cold sitting there warm and snug on my father's sheepskin coat! Before supper was over, Denny had fallen asleep at the table. Momma woke him and said, "Go to bed, Denny, before you fall off the bench."

Supper and dishes were scarcely finished when George and John were back in the kitchen looking for food to fill, as Momma and Daddy would say, "their hollow legs." Being healthy, growing young boys, their food intake was enormous. George ran outdoors to the garage and placed a stepladder under the gunnysack of popcorn that was suspended on a wire from a rafter. He brought in eight or ten ears of small white popcorn. Momma had a very large kettle in which she popped the corn, and the corn sounded like it was going wild when she shook the kettle on the stove. After it quit popping, she dumped it all at once into a dishpan on the kitchen table. I sat there waiting. Sometimes another kernel or two would pop and I would scurry to catch it before it hit the floor! John shook a little salt on the popcorn while it was still very hot. This process was repeated three or four times until the dishpan was full. One of the boys carried it into the living room where our dad sat reading the paper. Momma brought bowls for each of us to put our popcorn in. Then she tuned the radio to a play or a sing along. There we sat on the floor, contented, warm and cozy, happily eating popcorn and listening to the radio. When the program was over, Momma told me to go to bed. Under protest, I went.

The Sled

It was late February, and the heavy snow that had blanketed Perry was melting rapidly under a warm winter sun. I'd gone to the library to browse among the children's books. I'd read a number of them, but not all. I chose a few to read from, in the hopes of finding one that might catch my imagination. Kids always came and went through the children's section of the library. In fact, the librarian had to regularly shush us so we would not bother the other patrons at the tables in the larger room. Some of them would smile at us, but others would demand that the noisier children leave, so out the door they'd go, whooping and hollering.

This particular day it was getting close to four o'clock, so I put away the book I was looking at and left. I started walking east on Willis Avenue, then crossed over the street to the north side. Miller's Hardware sat facing the street on that side, and in one of its windows I saw something that caught my eye. There was a shiny Radio-Flyer sled with red runners and varnished wood. It was the most beautiful sled I'd ever seen! A sign tied to its front read $2, but this number had been crossed out and the sign now said, "Sale, $1." Wow! I had always wanted a sled all my own, but had never had one. And this one was just my size!

I ran the remaining ten blocks home, arriving there breathless. My excitement was almost more than I could withstand!

I entered the house without taking my coat or over-shoes off. I ran to the living room where my dad sat reading the evening paper.

"Daddy, Daddy!" I cried. "There is something I must tell you about. I saw it at the hardware store, and it's just my size, and it's only a dollar, can I have it please, Daddy, please?"

"Hey, slow down," he answered me. "What did you see at the hardware store?"

"I saw a sled, Daddy, just my size. It's the very last one they have and they only want one dollar for it! Please, can I have it Daddy, please?"

My dad said, "A dollar is a lot of money. It's twenty ice cream cones or one hundred suckers, or it's ten cakes of honey."

I stood still looking at my dad, puzzled at what he was saying to me. He continued, "If you really want the sled, you will have to earn the money. If you sell ten cakes of honey, you can keep the money and use it to buy the sled."

I only had six cents in my dresser drawer, not even close to the amount I needed.

I said, "I'll do it. Tomorrow's Saturday. I will go in the morning, first thing. Oh thank you, Daddy, thank you!"

I thought to myself, *Goodie, goodie! I'll have a sled of my own and Denny and I won't take the shovel to Haunted Hill anymore!*

Denny and I sat together on a bench on the far side of the table for supper. I told him about the sled. He wanted to know,

"Are there two? One for me, too?"

"No Denny, but I will share rides with you like we did on the shovel."

"But I want one of my own."

"I know Denny, but they only have one sled; I'll let you take turns with me."

He nodded his head yes and started to eat. As usual, he fell asleep at the table and had to be awakened to go to bed.

The next morning, I was up before eight o'clock, all scrubbed and dressed for breakfast. I noticed the little basket with the ten cakes of honey sitting on the dining room table. Over breakfast, Daddy inquired where I intended to sell the honey. He told me I was to stay close to home and not to cross the railroad tracks because that was George and John's area to sell honey.

It was still quite cold outdoors so I wore a scarf, a hat, and some mittens. I started off down Seventh Street stopping at all the neighbors' houses. I sold three cakes of honey there, and then moved on to Sixth Street where I sold three more. After heading west on Paul Street, I turned south onto Fifth Street. By that time it had started to warm up, and I could hear water trickling along the curb. My arm was hurting from carrying the basket so long. I had to be very careful—I didn't want to drop the four remaining cakes of honey.

(If a cake of honey gets turned over, then the honey will drain out of any unsealed cells. My cakes had been carefully placed in the basket so the incomplete cells would not drain out. Honey cells are sloped and point upwards. This honey was produced from plum tree blossoms and was clear like corn syrup. Most people enjoyed it and thought it to be a bargain at ten cents a cake. Because the cells in these cakes were not fully filled, my dad called them "culls," and we children were allowed to sell them door to door. The rest of the honey we wrapped in a cellophane and wax paper wrapper. Momma and Daddy took that honey to a wholesaler in Des Moines and sold it all at once.)

I was a little concerned that I may not be able to sell all of my honey. I stopped at one house next to the railroad tracks, and the woman asked me to step inside. She asked me to bring my honey to the kitchen table where her husband joined her. He placed a scale on the table and they proceeded to weigh each of the remaining cakes. Selecting the two heaviest, they carefully placed the last two back into my basket. The two dimes they gave me joined the other six already in my pocket.

Zigzagging across the streets, I walked a great distance for little legs before I sold the last two cakes of honey. In the end, I sold the last honey cake on North First Street, which was past Park Street, and a little farther away than Daddy intended for me to go. By the time I returned home, the hat, mittens, and scarf were rolled up in my little basket. I had to use the bathroom so bad I "twist-legged" my way into the house, shedding my coat and the basket on the floor, barely making it to the bathroom in time.

The family was waiting for me at the dinner table. I had a big smile on my face and Momma said, "I think Joyce has sold all her honey."

My dad said, "Her basket is empty. I'm surprised she came right home."

We bowed our heads and this time Daddy asked John to say the blessing. John said,

"WegivethankstotheeHeavenlyFatherforthisblessingweaskitinJesus'nameAmen."

Daddy said, "John, do you think you can say the blessing again, a little slower this time?"

John, not wishing to delay eating any longer, repeated the prayer clearly and in a most respectful manner.

Boy was I glad when he was done! Not only was I starved, but also I was in a hurry to leave for town. It didn't take me long to snarf down my food. My dad asked,

"Joyce, did you sell your honey?"

"Yes Daddy, and as soon as I eat I'm going to get the sled."

As I hurried towards town, I couldn't help but notice that the snow was mostly gone. My winter coat was far too warm so I unbuttoned it.

The sled was still in Miller's window. I tried and tried to open the latch on the door, but it just would not budge for my little fingers. I put my hands up by my eyes and peered through the glass. I could see a lady looking at me, so I knocked on the door. She came to the front of the store and opened the door for me.

"Excuse me, Ma'am. I want to buy the sled in your window."

"Come in, little girl. Didn't I see you looking through the window yesterday?"

"Yes'um. I asked my dad if I could have it and he gave me ten cakes of honey to sell to pay for it." I reached into my pocket and withdrew the ten dimes. "Here is my money."

She held out her hand and I placed the dimes in it. I don't remember receiving a sales slip. I just picked up the sled and she opened the door for me to leave.

I lived ten blocks from Miller's Hardware. After only two blocks the sled had become quite heavy to carry. As I had no rope or binder twine with which to pull it, I put the sled down on the walk and sat on it to rest. I was very tired.

Two blocks from home I discovered ice in the street. I tried to slide on it, but there was too much gravel mixed in. I thought, *Yesterday there was a lot of snow on the ground but today it's all gone. Don't know why it had to go so fast ... especially when I wanted to play in it!*

Arriving home, I carried it into the house and wiped the runners on the porch rug. My brothers were in the kitchen and were interested in my sled, but they kept telling me I would have to wait until next winter to use it.

"What do you mean wait till next winter?" I said.

"It's spring now, Joyce. We probably won't have any-more snow to slide on until next winter!" said George.

"Yeah," said John, "Why do you think it was on sale?"

"Cause it was the last one," I said.

"Yeah, I know," John answered.

Denny said, "The next time it snows, Joyce, I get first turn on your sled!"

I didn't recall promising him first turn, but did not say so. He could have first turn because there was only one sled for us. John and George shared a much larger sled, one far too large for Denny and me to handle.

My older brothers said my sled must be marked so I picked up the stove poker and slid it under a stove lid into the fire. I left it there until it was red hot. While waiting I thought, *Even if I don't get to use my sled anymore this winter, it will be ready to go next winter. I'll slide down Haunted Hill. I'll run and plop down on the sled and go farther down the street than anyone else has ever gone!*

I leaned the sled against the wall with the underside facing me. I removed the red hot poker from the fire and burned my initials—D.J.A.—on the underside. *Now,* I thought, *It really is mine, and no one can ever say it isn't!*

(Later Momma told me she and the clerk who waited on me at the hardware store had a laugh because my ten dimes were sticky. I thought to myself, *I wonder how they got sticky? Maybe the clerk was licking a sucker before I gave her the dimes.*)

Spring

Make Do Shoe Repairs

E very year I got new shoes in September. These were my school shoes, and they usually lasted until the following March. One evening in early spring, I removed my shoes to examine the soles because I had stepped on a small rock and my foot was hurting. I discovered a hole. I looked up at my dad who was reading and said, "Daddy, I've got a hole in my shoe."

"Let me see," he said, as he examined the sole. Then he asked me to put my shoes back on and stand while he poked around my toes.

"These shoes aren't worth repairing, Joyce," he said. "You need a new pair."

He sat back and resumed reading *The Perry Daily Chief*.

I went to the kitchen where John was eating a slice of bread dipped in cherry juice and sprinkled with sugar. (We kids thought this to be a treat!)

"John, I've got a hole in my shoe and it hurts when I step on a rock."

"Let me see it," he said. "Uh-huh. I can see it plain. Momma has a stack of empty matchboxes stashed in the cupboard. Go get a couple and bring the scissors."

I did as he asked and when I returned he had finished his bread. He said, "I'll show you how to fix this once but then you have to do it for yourself until you get a new pair of shoes. You're lucky your toes aren't all bunched up in them."

John got a pencil and drew a sole on one of the matchbox bottoms and cut it out. He slipped it into my shoe then removed it for further trimming. At last it fit snuggly in place. He traced around it and cut two more. He showed me how to fold and add additional cardboard pieces where the worn spot needed more padding. After placing all this in my shoe, he loosened my shoelace and said, "Put your foot in easy like so as not to bunch up your sock. How does it feel?"

"It feels fine. Thank you, John."

He said, "Now you have a pattern and can fix your own next time. Just don't use the matchbox tops. Momma sends them back to the company and they send us Teaberry chewing gum!"

"You mean like last summer when she gave each of us a stick every day?"

"Yes."

"Oh goodie! I'll never ever cut the tops."

The cardboard repairs lasted several days before another rock reminded me my shoes needed replacing. Then one day it rained on the way to school. The cardboard inserts completely disintegrated! And I wore a hole in my stocking. Momma carefully mended the hole with stocking thread, which looked a lot like embroidery thread. She took a length of it on a needle, pushed a used light bulb inside the sock under the hole, and sewed back and forth one way. Then, she rethreaded her needle and sewed the opposite direction, weaving in and out creating a fine woven patch over the hole. When I slipped the stocking on, it was as smooth as could be with no knots or lumps in it. I could not feel the patch! Then I noticed several more socks in her sewing basket needing repair. No wonder her work was more art than repair—she had so much practice with five children.

The following Saturday afternoon, Daddy took Momma, Denny, and me downtown in his 1929 Model A Ford pickup to Dennis Graney's shoe store. Mr. Graney fitted Denny and me with new oxford shoes. Mine were brown and Denny's were black.

Then Mr. Graney said, "Marion, Ruby, I have something to show you. It takes all the guess-work out of fitting shoes. It is called a 'fluoroscope.'"

He told me to step up to this machine and place my feet in the opening below. He looked into a viewing area and turned on the machine.

He said, "We have a perfect fit. Look, Ruby, you can see all the toes are straight and the ball of her foot is in place."

After Momma looked my dad took a look. Both agreed the shoes were a perfect fit and then they let me look. Wow! I could see all the bones in my feet from my arches to my toes.

"Step down Joyce, we want to check Denny's shoes," said Daddy.

Denny said, "I want to see first." He looked into the viewer and voiced his observation, "Those aren't feet—they're just bones!"

Everyone laughed and then checked the viewer and decided Denny's shoes were also a perfect fit. Then Mr. Graney turned off the machine.

Denny and I looked into the place where our feet fit and then into the viewing glass. Denny said, "I want to see my feet again."

Momma said, "No, Denny. It isn't necessary."

But Mr. Graney came over and turned the machine back on and Denny and I were allowed to once again see our feet. Soon our dad came over and told us to quit playing with the machine. He shut it off and made us sit until he and Momma were finished visiting with Mr. and Mrs. Graney. The next time I was in the store, the fluoroscope was gone. I don't know what happened to it. Perhaps it just stopped working.

The new shoes lasted me until school started in the fall. By then Momma had mended the shoelaces several times for me, and when her needle and thread could no longer repair the frayed laces, I tied knots in them. Sometimes our laces got to be so short they didn't reach all the eyelets in our shoes, but we still wore them. Many times during the thirties we had to "make do."

To Fly a Kite

One very windy Saturday in March I whined, "Momma, I ain't got nothin' to do. What can I do?"

Momma looked at me. "You what?"

"I haven't anything to do," I said.

Momma smiled. "Go outdoors to see what's going on in the garage."

I thought, *Oh boy, there must be something good going on out there. Why do I have so much trouble getting my coat buttoned up and my hat on?*

"Momma will you, excuse me, please will you help me with the new buttons on my coat?"

"I know they are tightly sewn to your coat, Joyce, but they will loosen some with use. There you go—all buttoned."

"Thank you, Momma!" I said, as I ran out the back door to the garage.

John and George were busy with some long pieces of lath. They had them wedged in the vise and were trying to saw small slits in their ends.

"Whatcha doin'? Whatcha makin'? Kin I help? Let me hold the lath," I said.

"Joyce," said George, "John is holding the lath, but when we are done he's going over to Chuck Havens'. Then you can help me. We are building a large kite."

I thought, *Goodie! He's going to let me help! George and John are good kite makers.*

The Saturday before he and John had made kites for me and Denny. We spent all morning trying to keep them in the air. It was lots of fun.

When they finished sawing, they measured down from the top to where they wanted the lath to cross, pounded in two nails, turned over the pieces, and pounded the nails into the wood so they wouldn't poke out and tear the kite.

John left. George let me help him carry the "frame" as he called it, to the front porch. He said I did a good job holding up the bottom end of the kite frame. I always liked to help George because he always needed me!

Momma came to the porch to help George wrap the twine around the frame. She said the kite was close to six feet tall, and she wondered if maybe they hadn't made it too large. "It will take a strong wind to get this off the ground," she said.

John had mixed up a jar of flour and water paste before he and George went to the garage. He had told me, "It has to stand a while to cure."

I didn't know paste had to "cure." I ate some paste at school one day and it tasted awful. Guess maybe it hadn't cured enough. I know the taste of it "cured" several of us from ever trying to eat it again!

When the paste was ready, Momma and George laid newspapers on the floor and pasted them together. Then they laid the frame on the paper and trimmed off the excess paper. I was disappointed they wouldn't let me help do any of this. After they folded the paper over the twine, they let me help paste and stick it down. George said I was a good paster-downer. Momma estimated how much tail they would need on "this contraption" as she called it. She chose heavier fabric for this kite than she did for the kites they'd made for Denny and me.

I wanted to take the kite out right away, but was told the paste had to dry before they could draw up the crosspiece like a bow and attach the twine on the back. Dinner was almost ready, and George thought the paste would be dry by the time we were done eating. He laid the kite on the front porch to dry. The sun was very warm shining through the storm windows on the porch. He was right; it was completely dry by the time we finished dinner.

Daddy came out to view our work, and was very surprised the kite was so large. He watched George and John draw up the crosspiece like a bow. The binder twine worked great. It tied very tightly to the lath and didn't slip. At last the colorful tail was added, and John and George carried the kite out the door. They let me hold the tail so it wouldn't get caught on anything.

The garden north of the house had been cleared the previous fall, so was a perfect spot to fly a kite. George held the big spool of binder twine while John carried the kite. When the wind gusted, John shoved the kite into the air and up it went about twenty feet, turned upside down, and landed on its top. We all ran to see if there was any damage. Thankfully, the kite didn't need any repairs. John decided it needed more tail to hold it upright. He ran to the house for more fabric, to which he also added his despised necktie! This time the kite soared into the air. The roll was spinning as George fed more and more twine to the airborne kite. The pull was increasing so John helped George hold the line.

What a wonderful sight—seeing that huge kite riding the air current far above our heads. It moved from right to left, sometimes up and sometimes down. When it started down, the boys would back up and pull on the twine and the kite would rise majestically. I could clearly see John's necktie whipping back and forth at the end of the tail. I was so excited I jumped up and down and squealed in delight, as only a child can express emotion! Some of the neighbors were standing in their yards looking up, and more than several neighbor kids came running to get a better look at George and John flying this enormous kite. What a thrill for all of us!

The Season of Long Winter Underwear

How we children looked forward to spring. One day in late April, we children shed our heavy winter coats as we walked home in the unseasonably warm sunshine. Dressing for school this time of year was a bit tricky, especially when most mornings were still very cool.

Momma always made me put on long-legged underwear each morning. Over this was placed a "pantywaist," which consisted of a series of straps girls put their arms through and stretched over their shoulders. One strap fastened around the chest and another fastened around the waist, from which dangled supporters for hose.

Each morning I would appear in the kitchen carrying my dress over my arm. There was never any need to put it on because I never learned to put on my pantywaist correctly, so the long winter underwear always bunched up around my legs under the cotton hose. Momma would have to remove the pantywaist from around my legs, turn it right side up, push my hose down, fold my underwear around my ankles, and pull the hose up over it without any wrinkles or bulges. Then she would fasten the supporters, which held up the hose. Whew! What a job to get a Kindergartner off to school.

When I was a little older, we girls would unfasten our stockings on warm days and fold them neatly over and over down our legs to our ankles. We carefully folded the long winter underwear up and over our knees and hid it under the skirts of our dresses. I must admit my folding was not as neat as the older girls and often my long winter underwear was merely rolled up. Thus, I had quite a bulge above each knee under my dress. How I hated that long winter underwear! I had to wear it until I entered the eighth grade.

At that time Momma bought me undershirts and very long-legged underpants to wear. These, too, came down to my knees! But my skirts were long enough to cover my knees so they never showed. I never wore long cotton hose to school again. (I would never have admitted it at the time, but there were many days walking from Seventh and North to the high school on Tenth and Willis that it was so cold when the wind blew against my bare legs I wished for that long winter underwear!)

At our house, overshoes were another piece of required equipment, along with stocking hats, wool scarves, heavy mittens, and wool coats. I used to try to sneak out of the house without my hat and overshoes, only to have my dad call me back to put them on. I think he would have come after me if I didn't turn around and return home to put on the hated articles. Sometimes when it was time to go out for recess, the sun was gone and the weather had turned cold. Then I was glad I had my hat and overshoes on! I wondered, *How did Daddy know it was gonna turn cold?* I guess parents know everything.

John's Amazing Throw

A s children, Denny and I enjoyed getting into George's and John's stuff. One time we went upstairs to their room and took their rubber band guns. (A rubber band "gun" was a piece of wood cut in the shape of a gun stock and barrel. One snap clothespin was mounted on the end of the stock, held firmly in place by several rubber bands. To load the gun, one slipped a rubber band "shot" into the clothespin and stretched it over the end of the barrel.)

We took the guns outdoors and decided to shoot at a fencepost, which was about twelve feet in front of us. The rubber bands were half-inch wide strips that had been cut from a rubber inner tube. After several failed attempts and hand snaps, we finally got both guns loaded.

"Denny, you go first," I said.

He took careful aim and released the clothespin. His shot missed the post by about three feet.

"My turn," I said. My shot landed in the driveway— nowhere near the post!

We spent the next half hour or so reloading and trying to hit the fencepost, getting better with every attempt. Suddenly I looked up and saw George and John coming up the sidewalk.

"Denny! Here they come!" I whispered. "Come on. We've got to put the guns back before they see us!"

Quickly we scrambled into the house and up the stairs. Carefully we put the guns back on the dresser behind their door and tiptoed into my room. I grabbed my checker set, and told Denny to sit at the table. I set up the board and helped him set up the pieces. We pretended to be intent at playing a game.

George and John came upstairs and went to their room. They shut the door. Denny and I held our breath. If the guns were not just as they had left them, then they would know we had been into their stuff, and would come after us with blood in their eyes. Quickly their door opened. We heard their footsteps going downstairs.

"That's strange," I said.

Denny looked at me and said, "Maybe they hid something."

"Like what?" I asked.

"I dunno. Maybe something they don't want us to see."

Suddenly I was worried. "Denny, maybe they saw us and they're setting a trap for us."

"I'll go take a look downstairs to see where they are," he said.

We tiptoed quietly out of my room and started down the hall. With every step we took, the floorboards squeaked. Carefully, Denny snuck down the stairs to the landing and peeked around the corner. He went down a few steps and looked into the dining room. He quietly came back upstairs and said,

"It's quiet. No one's around."

"Where's Momma?" I asked.

"She's outdoors."

The coast being clear, we hurried into George and John's room.

"Let's look around to see if anything's different," I said.

We looked on top of the larger dresser, under the beds, and under their pillows. Nothing looked different. Then we turned our attention to the little dresser behind the door. The rubber band guns were as we had left them, but the bottom drawer was ajar.

"I wonder what they got in there," I said.

"Let's look," said Denny.

As I pulled open the drawer, something rolled around inside it!

"What'er you doin' in my room?" John yelled.

Denny and I hollered and practically jumped out of our skins. There were George and John blocking the door. Suddenly, I was really scared. I'd been warned about going into the boys' room and getting into their stuff. I had to think fast.

"What you got in that drawer?" I asked.

John shouted, "None of your business and you better get out of here before I tell on you!"

I piped up. "You better tell me or I'll tell Daddy you got something live in that drawer. I saw it move and I'm scared of it!"

"John," George said laughing, "let them see it. It won't hurt anything."

Reluctantly, John opened the drawer.

"What is that?" Denny said.

John picked up the round metal object. "It's a cannon ball. Mr. Shipper brought it home from World War I as a souvenir."

"What's it doing here?" I asked.

George said, "He loaned it to John to practice shot put for the school games."

(Every year in the spring, many students from the three elementary schools in town would compete in a tournament. Each student was allowed to participate in one sporting event with other students in his or her grade level. I always went out for the hip, skip, and jump. While I could easily beat the girls in my class, Blanche Woolsan from Roosevelt would stretch out her long legs and beat me every year!)

"Let me see it," I said.

John handed the cannon ball to me. It was so large I needed both hands to hold it.

"It's heavy," I said. "How much does it weigh?"

"More than the shot put ball at school. About sixteen pounds," he said.

We took it outdoors so John could show us how he would practice with it. He wasn't very good on his first throw; the ball didn't go very far.

"Let me try it," I said.

I held it in my right hand over my shoulder, but had to take a step backwards to keep my balance!

John practiced every morning before school and then again in the afternoon. Daddy noticed he was developing strength in his arm and poise in his delivery. Every week John was able to throw Mr. Shipper's cannon ball much farther and straighter than the week before.

Daddy commented, "John, if you keep this up you will throw the shot put ball away and they'll never find it!"

John was so amused with Daddy's statement that he grinned from ear to ear.

The day of the tournament arrived and John was ready and confident. His competition from Roosevelt and Lincoln did well, and received applause from those watching. When it was John's turn, he stepped forward, lifted the shot put ball up and down with his right arm, paused, raised his left arm forward as he lifted the ball over his right shoulder, and let it fly. To everyone's astonishment, he threw it an unbelievable distance! The kids and the teachers all stood there awestruck, with their mouths hanging open. They could not believe their eyes. John's throw was a full eight feet farther than the best shot! They had never seen the shot put ball thrown so far by an elementary student. The applause and ensuing congratulations came from all who were there.

That night John was grinning from ear to ear as he told Daddy and Mr. Shipper about his win.

"So, your faithful workouts paid off?" asked Mr. Shipper.

John beamed. "Yes sir! Thanks to your cannon ball!"

All three of them were laughing harder than I had ever seen any of them laugh. Daddy and Mr. Shipper both slapped John on the back and congratulated him.

"I knew you would do it," said Daddy.

Mr. Shipper added, "You're the champion!"

What a great day for John!

The Playhouse

When I was eighteen months old, my parents moved from 1902 Fourth Street (where I was born) to 1624 North Street. Attached to the house on North Street was an enclosed back porch that led to a small open porch on the east end. There was no door leading from the enclosed part to this extension. When I was older, this open porch became my playhouse. In it I had two small rockers, a chair made from an orange crate, a small square table that had been my great-grandfather's, and a little gray kitchen cupboard that a neighbor girl, Gail Goodwin, had given me. Because there were no steps leading to this little porch, and because my legs were too short to crawl up there, my father thoughtfully placed a very large flat rock on the south end so I could easily gain access to this wonderful place to play. But best of all, it was my very own!

More than one morning, Momma let me take my breakfast out to my playhouse to eat. One particular morning I had rice and milk in a little white bowl. Ever so carefully, I carried it out the back porch door, down the steps and around the big porch to my playhouse. I placed the bowl carefully on the floor before climbing the rock step. After I was on the little porch, I picked up my bowl of rice and placed it on the table, pulled up the orange crate chair, and settled myself to eat. It was such a lovely spring morning. I could feel the warmth of the sunshine on the side of my face. The air was sweet with the scent of plum blossoms, and I could hear the bees buzzing in their search for honey. It was almost musical. My world was peaceful and I was contented.

I had a little set of aluminum baking pans in my play-house, which I used to make mud pies, cakes, and muffins. When they were dry enough to handle, I would put my "baked goods" in the little cupboard. When the mud dried completely, they were quite fragile and would often crumble when touched. I saved them for tea parties with LaVonne McDevitt or with Denny. Usually my delicacies were in shambles after his rough handling. He was not always a polite guest, nor was he always a welcomed guest. Well-bred visitors don't throw your baked goods at a post to see if they can hit it!

My dad learned of my problem in keeping baked goods and gave me a method to make them more substantial. (Parents seem so wise; they can always solve the most pressing problems for a child!) Daddy showed me how to mix together concrete, sand, and water for my pastries. He showed me how to tell when they were set, and how to tap them out of the pan to finish baking in the sun. Using this method, my supply of baked goods soon overflowed my capacity to store them!

Many hours were spent in the playhouse with my friend LaVonne McDevitt and our dolls. We had tea parties and took turns serving and playing "hostess." What a treat when Momma would give us real tea that was left over from dinner! (In those days, "dinner" was eaten at noon and "supper" was the evening meal. "Lunch" was something the kids from the country carried to school in a sack or tin box.)

On March 17, 1933, my great-grandmother Phillips died. At her request, I was given a milk glass pitcher and six drinking glasses. They were all decorated with flowers and trimmed in gold. She kept them on her buffet in the dining room and each time I visited her I would look at them and admire them. Sometimes I even reached up and touched them lightly. If my dad saw me, he reprimanded me, but Grandma Phillips would sternly rebuke him.

Carefully I placed these items on the table in the playhouse. LaVonne and I carried the pitcher to the well, pumped water into it, and carried it back to the table. We poured each of us a glass of water and sat back, enjoying these new additions to the décor. We kept tossing the water out and refilling our glasses just to hold the pitcher and take turns pouring. Every evening I had to bring the set into the house because Daddy was afraid someone might take it if left outdoors.

When winter came, all my playhouse things were moved to my room upstairs. By the fall of 1933, I had only one glass left. And when I picked it up one day, the bottom fell off! I sat there looking at the broken glass and realized all I had left was the pitcher. I picked it up and carried it downstairs to ask Momma if she would keep it for me. (She did, and its still in the family today. Whenever I think of the pitcher, I remember my great-grandmother's thoughtfulness and the many hours of fun I had playing with it in my playhouse. I shall never forget her legacy to me.)

Mushroom Hunting

One day in early May proved to be sunny and warm. We had had enough rain to cause the ground to be moist and the grass to spring up lush and green. Even the trees were leafing out. Daddy decided the time was right to go mushroom hunting down by the Raccoon River. Several years before, he had purchased a five-acre lot of timber, which we used every fall for firewood. Art and Mary Schuhardt had a pasture that joined this small strip of land. Daddy decided that their pasture was the best place to look for mushrooms because the Schuhardts always made us welcome to walk in their timber. After exchanging pleasantries with them, we entered their pasture through a gate on the north side.

I said, "Momma, I wish we could stay longer with them. It's fun to listen to Daddy and Mr. Schuhardt laugh and talk. Sometimes they laugh so hard tears come in their eyes and they hold their sides!"

John and George were allowed to walk ahead, but Denny and I had to walk with Momma and Daddy. They were scrutinizing the grass, but Denny and I were looking for squirrels, rabbits, flowers, bugs, and bees. (We looked for the first three for fun, and the last two because we were afraid of them!)

Suddenly my dad said, "Stop Joyce, don't make a move!"

"Is something goin' to git me?" I squealed in fright.

"No, but look just in front of your feet. What is that just ahead of your shoe?"

I looked down. "I don't see nothing but a funny-looking toadstool."

"No it isn't. Look closely, what does it make you think of?"

I thought for a moment. "Why it looks like a little sponge like the big ones you have in the paint shop."

"Right. It's called a morel mushroom and that is what we are looking for. Be careful to reach for the stem with your fingers and gently pull it loose."

I hesitated. "Will it bite me, Daddy?"

"Of course not."

I took hold of the mushroom and pulled. "I got it, Daddy. Look, I got it all by myself!"

"Joyce, look at the mushroom closely. See the little holes in it? Feel how light it is, and smell it. This is a good mushroom to eat. If it was heavy and smelled bad, you would know it is not a morel and that it was not good to eat. It could make you very sick."

I placed the mushroom in a basket Momma was carrying and no longer looked for rabbits and squirrels. My eyes were glued close to the ground.

George and John found quite a few, but I didn't find any more. I did find a Dutchman's-breeches just coming into bloom. Daddy took his putty knife and dug it up and placed it in Momma's basket.

When we retuned home, George and Momma washed the mushrooms and soaked them to get all the little bugs out. While they were doing this, Daddy and I took the little flower and planted it under the spirea bush on the east side of the house. (Several times during the summer, Daddy told me to give it a little water, and there it thrived.)

Daddy and I returned to the house where Momma was preparing the mushrooms for us to eat. First she dipped them in whipped egg, then she rolled them in flour, and then sautéed them in butter. They smelled so good, we ate them right away. There were too many for us to eat that evening so Momma placed the remaining uncooked mushrooms in a crock, covered them with cold water, and set them in the icebox.

Momma told me that morels often appear like magic near dead elm trees. One afternoon they are not there, then the next day they are! I thought that over a bit. *If they spring up like magic, do they disappear like magic?* The next morning I just had to make sure they were still in the crock. I asked Momma about it, and she told me they did not disappear magically, and that they were still in the icebox. Well, I had to see for myself! When no one was looking I slipped out to the porch to the icebox to have a look. I almost spilled them when I lifted the lid to check. Momma heard the noise and came out to see what it was. I quickly closed the door, pushed the latch down, then ran out the back door!

The Value of a Penny

On Saturday, May 12, 1934, I learned a lesson that has remained with me all my life. That was the day I learned the value of a penny, and to this day I cannot step over one lying on the floor or sidewalk as others do. I always pick it up.

It was a cool, somewhat windy day, with sunshine peeking in and out of the clouds. I awoke unusually early, anxious to get started on my surprise gift for Momma for Mother's Day, which was the following day. I had been saving and planning for her gift a long time. Slipping quietly out of bed, I tiptoed to my dresser and for the umpteenth time opened the little powder container to count the fifteen pennies I had saved one by one. There were eight Indian heads and seven Lincoln heads. They were bright and shiny and caught the sunlight as I moved them around in the container. Each one had been laboriously shined by hand on an old wool rug before they were placed in the powder box for safekeeping. Carefully I replaced the lid and returned the box to its place on my dresser.

That day had to have the longest morning I could ever remember. I had been told that after lunch my dad would take me with him to downtown Perry. (He often took me on warm Saturdays to meet my friend Dorothy Meier. Dorothy and I would talk, laugh, giggle, and exchange important news with all the other kids who had come to town with their parents. Sometimes we even received a nickel for a sack of popcorn, an ice cream cone, or a fountain drink from the drugstore. Sitting on a counter stool at the drugstore drinking a cherry cola was a good sign you were grown-up even if you are only nine years old.)

After lunch, I hurried to my room, took a hanky from my drawer, and spread it open on the dresser. I lifted the glass lid from the powder box and poured the pennies onto the corner of my hanky. Once again they were counted, made into a little stack, and the hanky securely knotted. I was now ready to go to town!

My dad parked his 1929 Model A Ford pickup diagonally on Main Street. He told me if he wasn't back by half past four, I was to walk home. I looked around Perry for my friend Dorothy but couldn't find her. Perhaps her folks weren't coming to town this week. Sometimes they didn't, but the day before Mother's Day was always a big day in town. Not being able to locate her, I hurried to Woolworth's Five and Ten Cent Store to see what exciting gifts were being offered for Mother's Day. I started at the counters closest to the front door. I looked at all the jewelry, candy, ribbons, Lady Esther face powder, and cold cream. There was Jergen's and Chamberlain's hand lotion, and Evening in Paris, Gardenia, Blue Waltz, and Radio Girl perfume. Also there was Fitchs' Dandruff Shampoo, Rose Hair Oil, Bay Rum Aftershave, as well as many hairnets, hairpins, combs, powder puffs, emery boards, and fingernail care sets.

Oh, what a beautiful, bountiful selection from which to choose, and none of it over ten cents!

I kept walking until I came to the rear of the store where there were blouses, children's dresses, underclothes, anklets, hosiery, and garters. I looked up from the display counter and there before my eyes dangling from a hanger was the most beautiful apron I had ever seen! It had a floral design on a white background with matching aqua bias trim. The tie belts were fastened at the waist and tied into a very full bow in the back. It was beautiful! I just knew this apron was the special Mother's Day gift for which I had been searching, yet it was so pretty it probably was much too expensive for me to purchase.

A clerk saw me standing there and asked, "May I help you?"

I answered, "Please tell me how much the apron is."

She looked at the little ticket dangling on a string pinned to the pocket, turned to me and said, "It's fifteen cents."

Only fifteen cents! And I had just enough money to buy it. Happily I told her I would take it. She removed it from the hanger, folded it, placed it in a sack, and said, "Sixteen cents, please."

I looked at her for a moment. "You told me it was fifteen cents."

She replied, "There is a one-cent sales tax on it."

Tax! I had heard something about a sales tax being put into effect discussed among my parents and their friends. A sales tax had nothing to do with me, or so I thought.

"But I've only fifteen cents to spend—"

"I'm sorry, little girl. You must have the penny tax for the apron."

With that, she removed the apron from the sack and replaced it on the hanger. My disappointment became a knot in my stomach as I watched a woman ask to see the apron. Much to my relief, she decided it was not what she wanted and left it lying on the counter as she walked away.

The town clock, which hung from the First National Bank Building on First and Willis Avenue, said 3:30 PM and that meant I had one hour to find my dad before I had to go home. It was Daddy's habit of talking with various businessmen each week about their painting and papering needs. He often traded work with them for school books, shoes, eyeglasses, groceries, and dental care. I looked in Ainley's Bookstore, Bert McLaughlin's Grocery, Bill Tack's Denniston & Partridge Lumber Company, Ray B. Smith's Drugstore, and Dennis Graney's shoe store, all to no avail.

Up and down the street I walked looking for my dad. I just couldn't find him! (I did not know my dad was filling in that afternoon for a bartender at the Elks Club.) Time was slipping by and if I didn't find him soon, I would have to forget about the apron with its pretty flowers and trim and settle for a powder puff or hanky for Momma. She would have looked so nice wearing that apron with her light brown hair and blue eyes. And all for the lack of one cent!

Just last week my little brother Denny and I had gone to the neighborhood store to buy two suckers for one cent, my treat. How I wished we hadn't gone! I would have had the penny I needed so badly now. I had never realized until now how important money could be. It meant whether one could or could not have something one desired or even needed.

Suddenly someone said, "Hello, Joyce."

I looked up. It was my great-aunt Daisy Steward. (She had such dark brown eyes. She was my Grandma Anderson's sister. I never knew my Grandma Anderson because she died before I was born.)

Forgetting to be courteous and politely say hello to my great-aunt, I blurted out, "Have you seen my dad?"

"Why no, child," she answered, "I haven't seen him. Is there something wrong?"

I told her about the apron, my fifteen cents, my great need for one more penny for the tax, how I couldn't find my dad, how my time uptown was almost gone, and how Mother's Day was tomorrow.

She interrupted me to say, "Well, if that's all you need, I can help you."

To my surprise, she opened her big purse, rummaged in it momentarily, and handed me the penny I needed for the tax. I was so happy and relieved I couldn't thank her enough.

Quickly I returned to the dime store. I couldn't run in the store so I walked as fast as I could to the counter where the apron hung. But it wasn't hanging there anymore! There was a pink one hanging in its place. The apron was gone! Someone else had bought it. The tears welled up in my eyes. It took me too long to get the penny for the tax!

The clerk at the counter turned around, saw me and said, "I see you're back. I thought you probably would be, so I saved the apron for you."

She pulled the apron from beneath the counter, placed it in a sack, took my fifteen shiny pennies plus one very dull, black penny for the tax, and handed me the package. At last I had Momma's Mother's Day gift! I tightly held the sack in my hand as I went out the door. Just then the town clock chimed half past four and it was time for me to walk home.

(Sales tax went into effect April 1, 1934, at the rate of 2 percent.)

Memorial Day, 1934

As I lay awake in bed listening to the birds chirping outside my bedroom window, I remember what day it is. I roll over to look outside the window to make sure the sun is shining. With my forehead pressed against the glass, the early morning sun is warm upon my face. I look down at the driveway and the iris bed that lines it. Delicate blossoms in full bloom, they are white, yellow, lavender, and deep purple. My favorite iris has three flowers opening on it; they are white with lacy lavender edges. I've watched the irises all week hoping they would bloom for today. Momma will probably let me pick them because I like them so much. The peony bushes are heavy with large flowers, some so heavy they lay on the ground. I will have to be careful not to step on them and crush them—or maybe break the stems too short—because Momma would be disappointed to lose such beautiful flowers.

I see a kitty coming up the driveway. It's the grey and black tiger I've seen my youngest brother David playing with. He gives it pieces of his bread and butter every morning as a treat. Momma has told him to leave the kitty alone, but David likes to hold it and the kitty doesn't object to being unceremoniously draped over David's arm and wagged around. (Eventually he was allowed to keep the cat and it was named Miss Ritzey.)

I hear Momma stirring in the kitchen getting breakfast. Soon I smell bacon and coffee. I decide to get up and go downstairs to the kitchen. Maybe I'll be first up. I'm too late. As usual, Denny is the first to wake up and go downstairs! While I'm "washing up," I hear George and John coming down the stairs. They've got David with them and he's chattering excitedly because they have told him where we are going and what we are planning to do today.

We assemble at the breakfast table. Daddy sits at one end, and Momma at the other in front of the stove. Next to the wall sits Denny, then me, then David. Across the table sits John and George. We wait for Daddy to say the blessing.

Finally he speaks. "We give thanks to Thee, Heavenly Father, for this blessing. We ask Jesus' help through this day. Amen."

Momma serves pancakes to Daddy first, then to each of us children. Daddy has passed the bacon so David does not whimper while waiting for his pancake, but sits quietly munching on the crisp bacon. For our pancakes, Momma has made syrup from sugar and water (our favorite over honey or sorghum).

When breakfast is over we all go outdoors to pick the flowers to take to the cemetery. George and John get the buckets from the barn and fill them half full of water. George and Momma do most of the flower picking while John gets the vases we will use at the cemetery. John is very brave; they are in the basement and he is not afraid of the spiders that live down there. The rest of we children run around trying to keep out of the way. Momma calls me to come pick my three flowers. She shows me where to cut the stems so they will be the right length. My dad cuts roses from an early bush and places them in water. (He does this every year and puts them on his mother's grave. The bush is one his father gave his mother years ago. After Grandpa Anderson died, my dad dug up the bush and planted it in our yard next to the driveway by the iris bed.)

The buckets full of flowers are lifted by my dad and placed on the back seat floor of our 1924 Willys Knight touring car, an open air job with no windows. (It had heavy black curtains with isinglass inserts for windows that were snapped onto the car from the outside when it rained or was too cool.) George and John sit in the back seat with the box of vases between them. Denny and I sit on the front seat between Daddy and Momma. David sits on his favorite perch—Momma's lap.

Daddy slowly eases the car out of the driveway and heads east to Eighth Street, then turns north to Violet Hill Cemetery. There is a rut in the gravel road and the vases rattle in the back and the boys howl that the water is spilling. There are many cars on the road plus the people walking and carrying their flowers and containers. It's a busy day for everyone.

Our first stop is the graves of Grandad George and Grandma Hattie Anderson and Uncle Bob Thompson. (I remember my Grandfather Anderson used to send me to his little neighborhood store to buy cheese crackers. I also remember seeing him sick in bed a few days before he died. There were wooden planks on each side of him that were run through the foot and head of his bed to keep him from falling out. I was born in his house, as were George and John. Our grandmother Hattie died long before any of us were born.) Daddy digs a hole for his jar of roses in front of this mother's headstone. Momma carefully arranges the flowers in the vase. So many people are here this morning, and everyone stops to talk with us. We've seen Mrs. Hawk, Mrs. Daniels, Miss Stoner, Mrs. Havell, Mrs. Fink, Mrs. Foote, and on and on the list could go. My brothers and I speak politely to everyone, addressing them as Mr., Mrs., or Miss. Coming to the cemetery is sort of an exciting annual trek for us children, but a respectfully somber observance for the adults.

About this time Aunt Orpha arrives. She is riding with Mae Brown in her little coupe. She is pleased with the flowers Momma has placed on Uncle Bob's grave. (My uncle Bob Thompson, with a gun, took his own life in the basement bathroom of the Post Office where he was employed. The old Post Office building on Third and Warford now houses the School Administration offices.) Dramatically, my aunt sniffs a little and blows her nose.

Our next stop is on the east side of the old cemetery at the graves of Great-grandfather Shubbal and Great-grandmother Margaret Phillips. (I remember my dad and I would stop on the way home from Sunday school to visit Grandma Phillips. I don't remember many conversations with her, but she used to let me play her beautiful old organ that was in the dining room.)

(When Grandma Phillips had died the previous spring, she was brought home in her black casket and placed in the front bedroom of her house for viewing. It had been raining the day we called. I remember all we children were lined up at the door waiting to enter. My great-aunt Daisy opened the door and asked if the children's feet were clean. This upset Momma because she taught us to always clean our feet before entering a home. The consequences for not observing this ritual were too costly for us to forget! Momma assured Aunt Daisy our shoes were properly wiped, as evidence on the porch rug showed. We entered the bedroom and I looked down into the face of this little woman who had such white hair and looked like she was asleep. I did not realize what death entailed; at that point in my life, my only brush with death had been when Denny and I buried a dead bird in a shoebox under the plum trees. We later dug it up to see if it was still there or if it had gone to heaven. Momma scolded us for doing this, so we reburied it. Somehow I don't think they dig up people like that.)

Quietly I stand looking down at the red stone that says 'Mother.' This is where that tiny woman whose red hair turned snow white but whose beautiful light blue eyes never faded, now lies. I go to the large stone that says 'Phillips' on one side, and has Grandma and Grandpa's names, birth, and death dates on the other. The inscription which Denny and I read says, "At Rest." Momma and Daddy and Aunt Orpha arrange the flowers, while George has David in tow, and John checks out the ground squirrel holes.

Being finished at the Phillips gravesite, with a few flowers and vases left we walk to the road, get into the car, and head towards Fairview Church Cemetery. We drive north of Violet Hill to the turn at Bess' corner and then down the hill across Beaver Creek over Black Bridge. The bridge still scares me so I don't look down into the water below. We wind around north through the countryside and soon arrive at Fairview. George and John carry what is left of the flowers and the vases down the hill to the northwest edge of the cemetery where my Great-grandfather Robert and Great-grandmother Charity Anderson are buried. (Robert was a circuit rider preacher for the Methodist Church under Peter Cartwright.)

Finished here, we walk uphill a ways to the Van Lanningham marker. (These were my dad's aunts. One Anderson girl married a Van Lanningham and had three sons: Stacy, who became an auctioneer, Alonzo, who became a barber, and Elby, who became an attorney. Their mother died and their father married their mother's sister. This union produced one son named Harry who was a restaurateur. The first Mrs. Van Lanningham's stone has an interesting engraving that says, "Mother, we miss you at home.")

All flowers in place, all visiting with others finished, we get into the car for a leisurely drive home in time to watch the Veteran's parade march down our street towards Violet Hill Cemetery.

School's Out!

The last day of school always fell just before Memorial Day. We cleaned out our desks, took our books in our arms, and headed out the door. As we crossed the playground, we chanted, "School's out, school's out! No more pencils, no more books. No more teacher's cross-eyed looks!"

Each year we were responsible to acquire our own school books. If a new book had been introduced that year in the grade ahead of us, we would ask someone who had one if they would sell it. Most of the time we could buy our books this way for less than half the price. Since there were four school children in my family, books were always handed down. Usually by the time my younger brother Denny was finished with them, they needed to be discarded. (It wasn't until I was in the eighth or ninth grade that the school began buying all our books from us, and after that we paid a flat rental fee for them every year.)

On the Monday following Memorial Day, we always returned to the school to pick up our report cards. One year I arrived at the school a little early in order to play on the swings, but found they had all been removed. The giant slide, the teeter-totters, and the merry-go-round were gone! (It was the custodian's job to take down all this equipment every summer and paint, repair, and store it until school opened in the fall.) The only things left were the three bars that were anchored in the ground. I swung my leg over the middle bar, and sat there until Betta Small came along and joined me. Soon Lorraine Bennett, Ethel Anfinson, Betty Hall, and Jean Krohn, among others, also came. There we waited for Mr. Callahan, the custodian, to unlock the doors of Webster School and allow us to enter.

When he did, we lined up single file to march into the building and to our classrooms. We took what had been our assigned seats and waited for the teacher to pass out our report cards. The teacher always dismissed us in an orderly manner, but on our way out we would ask one another, "Did you pass?" The answer was always, "Yes. Did you?"

When I was in the fifth grade, I lingered in the hallway until it cleared. I then entered my teacher's room. Only a few days before Miss Covey had confiscated my yo-yo. I was innocently looking at it when it slipped from my fingers and unrolled, which meant I had to jerk it back up. Even though I wasn't playing with it, and hadn't broken any rules, she took it from me and placed it in her desk.

I approached Miss Covey and said in my most repentant voice, "I'm sorry I was playing with my yo-yo in class. Please may I have it back?"

She opened the drawer, picked it up, and handed it to me.

"Thank you," I said, and quietly left.

All the way home I played with my yo-yo. I was happy to have it back. My thoughts, however, were on the pleasures of summer vacation and all the fun yet to come. It was sort of bittersweet, though, knowing I would not see some of my friends again until fall.

The Andersons, 1930
Left to right: back row, George and John; *front row,* Ruby, Dennis, Joyce, and Marion

The Anderson children at 1624 North Street, summer 1935
Left to right: back row, George and John, *middle row,* Dennis and Joyce, *front row,* David
(This was the last photograph taken of David. He died shortly before his third birthday from complications after sustaining burns in an accidental backyard fire.)

About the Author

Joyce Anderson Halling was born and raised in Perry, Iowa. After graduating from Perry High School in 1942, Joyce worked full time as a clerk at F. W. Woolworth's dime store. From August of 1942, until its closing in August of 1945, she worked at the Ordnance Plant in Ankeny manufacturing war materials.

On December 2, 1945, she married Bill Halling and moved to a farm southwest of Perry. Their daughter Debbie was born in 1949, and their daughter Shelley in 1950. For eleven years Joyce worked at the Woodward State Hospital-School (now the Woodward Resource Center) in their Handicraft department, where she taught knitting, crocheting, and needlework. In 1984, Bill and Joyce moved back to town and Bill retired from farming in 1986.

Over the years Joyce has enjoyed a variety of work including raising chickens, feeding hogs, and sewing everything from dance costumes to fur coats. She's plastered and painted walls, hung wallpaper, upholstered furniture, and laid carpet.

Today, Joyce still enjoys handiwork, as well as writing, and visiting with her granddaughter and her great-grandson.

Although Joyce has traveled extensively throughout North America, Europe, and the Middle East, she still thinks the best place to be is in Perry, Iowa.

After Bill's death in 1997, Joyce continued to live in Perry until August of 2005. She now makes her home in Wilton, Iowa.